DESIGN
your home

Shaynna Blaze is a qualified interior designer who has created stunning interiors in residential and commercial spaces for over twenty years. Shaynna has been a finalist in the Australian Interior Design Awards and her designs have been featured internationally in design magazines and publications such as *1000 Global Interiors*. Shaynna is also a resident expert and presenter on LifeStyle Channel's award-winning *Selling Houses Australia* and a judge on Channel 9's popular home makeover show *The Block*.

DESIGN
your home

SHAYNNA BLAZE

PHOTOGRAPHY BY VANESSA HALL

VIKING
an imprint of
PENGUIN BOOKS

CONTENTS

INTRODUCTION

Whether your home is grand or humble, whether you own or rent makes no difference; it doesn't matter who or where you are, we all want the same thing: a home we love to live in.

Glossy high-end magazine pictures entice us with how our homes *could* look, but more often than not we close the pages with a sigh, and we're left wishing. Wishing for a lottery win so that we'd be able to do up our homes in the way we've always dreamt of. Wishing we had the time to tackle the task, or wishing we knew exactly what that elusive 'secret ingredient' was which would make our homes just *work*.

I'm here to tell you, these ideals are not out of anyone's reach. It's all about defining how you live; after that, the right space will follow.

As an interior designer, I'm here not just to make your home 'pretty' but to solve problems and find solutions. A decorator adds colour and gives visual impact to your interior. An interior designer does this as well, but their main responsibility is to design the space as a whole. An interior designer will be thinking about everything from how you walk around a room, where you're likely to sit and what goes in which drawer through to issues like natural versus artificial light, general comfort and how you want to live in your home now and in the future. A lot to consider, isn't it? An interior designer creates an individual space that is unique to you, and one that is not only beautiful but functional, and will remain so for years to come.

To me, the interior of a client's home is like a book of blank pages. Before I can help to fill it in, I have to get inside the person's head, to find out what's most important in their life. Then I work with their story till their ideal home appears in my mind like a 3-D pop-up book. This has taken me years of practice, years of listening to problems and hearing, 'Why is it *so hard*?', 'Where do I start?' and, 'How do you do it?'

Want to know why it's so hard? You are focusing on the wrong things.

Want to know where to start? Learning about the rules of interior design will help you to make the right decisions for the space you want to improve (and they're not as tricky to master as you think).

How do I do it? Well, I'm about to show you.

We all want to express our individual style and have our homes look as though they were put together effortlessly. That's all well and good, but no small – let alone great – event happens with out proper planning and thorough execution. If you go to a fantastic party and all you talk about the next day is the fabulous food you ate, the music you danced to, and how some people's outfits weren't doing them justice, then what you really witnessed and took part in was a smashing success. You didn't say how long you had to wait for snacks or drinks, how long the line was for the toilet or how the music really didn't suit the occasion, because behind the scenes the operation ran like clockwork. An idea was struck on, a formula was set and the execution was flawless. Can you see the link? If you can't, then you *really* need this book.

Brace yourself now, as I'm about to say a couple of swearwords when it comes to interior design:

research, planning and rules. Are you horrified yet? Interior design seems to be all about unrestrained freedom of expression, and that's definitely part of it, but as with many other creative pursuits, you've got to know what the rules are before you can have fun with them.

So, the good news is that rules are meant to be broken. Once you've got a firm idea of why interior designers look to certain guidelines when it comes to creating proportion, balance, harmony and contrast in a room, you can then throw caution to wind and achieve that truly individual interior you are dying to have.

This is getting personal, isn't it? Well, it should be! Your home is about you, your life and those you invite into your space.

Every time my door is opened, whether by a friend, colleague or a photographer from a magazine, I feel pressure to have my home be the epitome of style and glamour – the sort of place that everyone should aspire to have. Being judged based on my home's appearance is the lot of the interior designer. That sort of anxiety is enough to make anyone break into a cold sweat, but I don't expect my clients to live with that same burden – and I tell them that: your house needn't look picture-perfect every day. And yet, everyone has to bear one set of expectations or another. In our minds, we all carry an idea of what we expect our house to look like, but we don't let ourselves dream about how to make the most of the house we are expected to live in.

Our homes should be about being real and honest in how we live, rather than trying to attain a way of living that we aren't comfortable with or doesn't suit us. My home is on show not only because I am a designer, but because I'm a mother, a wife, a friend and, most of all, me. Our house will always be a place where family and friends gather for barbecues, dinner parties and afternoon chats over cups of tea.

Being a designer is, of course, a huge part of my life: I live and breathe it. I love it and make it a part of everything I do, but my profession doesn't

define every other person in my house… they have to live here too.

I have always dreamt of residing in a 1920s Hollywood-style glamourous mansion with rich black timbers and silken surfaces. I see it all so clearly: there I am, walking around in my flowing robe and kitten heels. I'm reading my book while lounging seductively on my perfect chaise, looking up only to ponder which exotic locale I will travel to next, first-class, of course.

Screeeech! – and then, yes, I wake up from my dream.

So what does my actual home look like? It is exactly that: a home. It has been bumped and scarred and very much lived in by my husband, two kids, a border collie and me.

What I dream of and how I live are completely different. My husband and son are sports nuts, and day in, day out we get wet bikes through the front door and smelly sports gear dragged around. My daughter flies in like the Looney Tunes' Tasmanian Devil, dropping one bag (and leaving it there, by the way), filling up the next, shouting 'Bye!'

as she grabs a quick snack from the fridge and disappears before we can catch our breaths to say, 'What was that?' Me, I'm always in a hurry to get to some appointment or to head to the airport. I always have a number of suitcases opened, ready to be filled and/or emptied, and each day I leave the house with a minimum three different types of bags. My home has to cope with items being dragged in or bounced down the stairs and still look great at a moment's notice if someone is 'just around the corner' or rings the doorbell mid-crisis.

My house isn't perpetually showroom-ready, but because each room works the way my family and I need it to in our daily lives, I can get the house up to 'inspection standard' in close to half an hour. And, no, that doesn't mean every spare cupboard is filled to the brim, on the cusp of having the entire contents fall out at any moment! I learnt long ago that your space has to work with you, not against you. Getting the house up to par certainly isn't effortless – I still have to run around like a mad woman for about thirty minutes – but it's achievable.

Mistakes? Oh, there have been a few, but for as long as I can remember I've loved experimenting, and it's taught me so much. When I first did up my bedroom at the tender age of fifteen, I wanted to cover my walls with vintage film posters from the 1920s and 1940s (I have been dreaming of that era for a long time). I didn't have enough posters to cover two walls so I raided the pantry and used tinfoil. Who needs wallpaper anyway? I knew that glamourous houses always had timber floors so I removed the carpet. Streamlined window treatments with white metal venetians? Check! (Actually, the venetians were already there, and as we didn't have the money to replace them, I convinced myself they were perfect.) My room looked great. Except when winter came, I froze. The only heating was in the lounge room at the other end of the house and my room was now filled with hard reflective surfaces. I still remember to this day how my teeth chattered even as I lay there with the bedclothes tucked up to my chin.

What it taught me was that surfaces make a huge difference in terms of comfort, and putting your bed next to a wall of tinfoil and under the window does not make for a happy, warm night's sleep. I couldn't bear the thought of removing my posters. I'd glued the posters to the walls (these were the days before Blu Tack) and taking them down meant they'd be lost to me forever. I suffered through two frigid winters like that, but my room looked amazing. It goes to show how people will put up with something that makes their life miserable if it looks good.

That said, you can also go too far the other way. The fear of trying something different or making a mistake can freeze us into putting up with what we have, even if it isn't working for us. With some of my clients I can see a 'paralysis of analysis', and over-thinking matters out of the fear of not getting it right can sometimes mean you do nothing at all!

Every time you open your front door, you get the chance to reflect on what about your home makes you happy. What's the first thing you think after you open the door when you come home? The greatest thing a client has ever said to me was, 'Now every time I walk into my house I can't help but smile.' Another client said, 'It's just a pleasure to come home to every day.' Why? Because their home is about them; it reflects who they are and how they see their lives.

I want you to feel that exact same way. And I'll show you how to create a place to call home.

It's all about recognising how we live and appreciating those we share our lives with, so that every space in the home works equally well for everyone.

The first step is to break things down room by room, as I do in this book. Even though it's a simple idea, thinking of each living space individually can throw people into such confusion; most get caught up in the so-called major decisions like, 'Which of these 75 shades of white do I really, *really* have to have?' Focusing on the bigger picture is far more important. You can apply the same basic principles of design to your whole house, but truly understanding the different spaces means recognising that each room has its own set of rules. We will look at each living space to see the ways you can change it to work for everyone in your family. Your life will shape the flow of the space and determine which elements you need to consider to be able to make it all work in your daily life.

Rules give structure to help us cope with life's daily chaos. This means if you follow my rules for your interior spaces, it doesn't matter how much your life gets out of hand, it won't take you long to get it all back under control. Now, that *has* to make you smile.

Shaynna

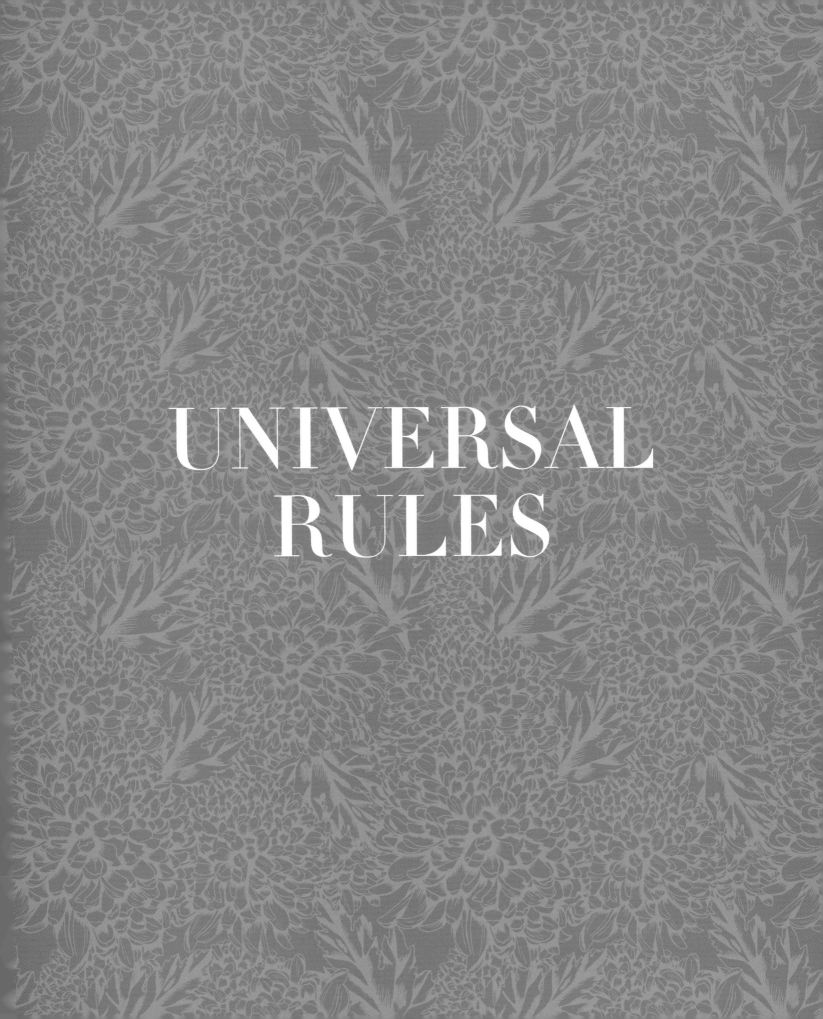

UNIVERSAL
RULES

UNIVERSAL RULES

Each room and space has individual rules that work for it, but there are universal rules that will always apply. Some are more relevant to certain areas in the house but you can take a little from all of these principles to help you with any room.

- **SCALE:** Get the proportions right – from the size of the furniture to how much room the accessories take up.
- **PLACEMENT:** Create the right flow in a room by taking into consideration the windows, doors and the type of furniture you need to make the best use of your space.
- **SHAPE:** Angular, fluid or boxed, the shape of your interior will influence the outcome of your style.
- **NUMBERS:** Pairs or groups of items set a certain mood and structure when you are decorating.
- **THE ODDS AND EVENS:** How you place your items on a shelf or scatter your cushions on the couch gives you the recipe for creating a formal or informal décor.

A very simple rule is: pairs equal 'bookends'. This means everything is contained in a neat, structured package. Bookends aren't just there to hold books up but to give a 'beginning' and 'end'; bookends signal 'this is as far as it goes'. So when you are putting a décor item, say, at each end of a shelf, you are creating a 'contained' visual look. Formal environments are all about elegance but also about focus. Creating even 'bookends' in an interior means the eye stops and takes time in

that one spot before it moves on. It might sound strange but when you force the eye to stop in one spot you create a sense of calm, and a formal room is about slowing down and taking the time to take it all in.

A formal room is about slowing down and taking the time to take it all in.

Uneven numbers equals room to move. An informal atmosphere is like a free spirit, giving permission to roam and take things in at your own pace. Uneven items look great in a group, as they capture the eye but at the same time give licence to scan each individual item within the group. Having a group of three cushions that are different patterns or colours is playful and suggests a certain confidence, as well as an inviting atmosphere. I guarantee if a room has two couches, one with three cushions stacked to one side and the other with a perfectly placed cushion at either end, you'll definitely gravitate towards the first one. Odd numbers create an inviting and casual environment that says 'come join me'.

Simply by arranging your cushions in different ways, you can give a completely different feel to your interior. Play around with cushions on your couch in even and odd placements, as in these examples, and see if you get a different reaction when people walk into the room.

CIRCLES AND SQUARES

Straight lines, squares and rectangles add up to a formal and strong interior look. But if you overdo it, you can be in danger of creating a hard, uninviting space.

Circles and curved lines are relaxed and informal, creating a more 'organic' feel within a space. If overused these can suggest that your space – or even you – aren't to be taken seriously, or else they can make a room feel too busy.

The key, as always, is to create balance.

SIZE IS EVERYTHING

'We have a huge room so we need to get really, really big furniture to fill it, right?'

'I think I have the smallest room in the whole world and it's going to take a potion from *Alice in Wonderland to shrink my furniture so I can fit everything in it! Right?'*

Just like *Alice in Wonderland* these quotes are complete fantasy, so get off whatever Lewis Carroll was on and keep reading.

Whether your room is large, small or odd-shaped, it is about creating a sense of balance. There is no use having a huge room full of oversized furniture if all or one person in your family is five foot three – every time they sit down their legs will dangle like they are back in preschool. How do I know? I'm five foot three, and I know from experience that some chairs are just plain humiliating!

Getting the right mix of large and small pieces is not only about creating balance in terms of the size of the room – making sure everything will fit – but also achieving balance visually. This includes not just your furniture but everything else in the room too: artwork, rugs, vases, statues, and so on. You have to treat each piece as part of the same family, and everyone needs to get along.

This lounge room is huge and to try to fill it without making it look overstuffed was always going to be a challenge.

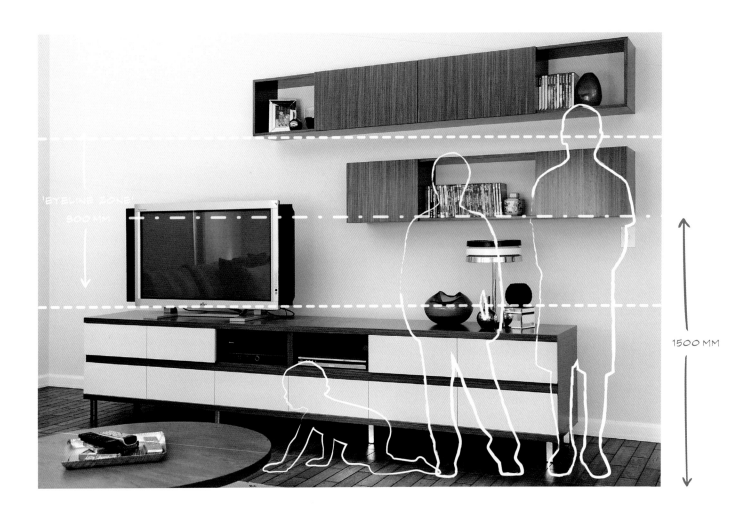

1500 MM

THE MIDDLE CHILD

Think of the pecking order in a family of three kids. The eldest child seems so much more grown up and self-sufficient than the others; the youngest child always there, hanging around at your feet; and then there's the middle child, who tends to miss out on the attention, despite their craving it. Sometimes they have to do something extraordinary to try to stand out.

When you walk into a room, your eye will nearly always be drawn to whatever sits directly at that level: whatever is most clear in your eyeline will be the first thing to catch your attention. The eye follows a natural line and the first things you see will be in this zone.

As I said, I am five foot three, but my husband is six foot three. Even in stilettos I will never reach his height: our eyeline levels are quite different. So in interior design, we use a standard eyeline to guide us when creating visual balance. The starting point for your eyeline is 1.5 m, and the eyeline 'zone' sits 400 mm above and below that. Realistically, you have an area of 800 mm to play around with, to capture the eye's attention, so keeping focus in this zone with your artwork, accoutrements and so on, will give you the most impact when creating a focal point.

When you have an object like a lamp around the eyeline height, it is important to keep a fluid look to it and not have other pieces like tall cabinets and low stools sitting outside the eyeline zone.

Just like the middle child, one thing in the room is going to want to stand out. But it has to be at the right height and have the right shape and composition to suit the area. Even if you only have three things together and their heights are jumping in and out of the eyeline zone, that will instantly create visual unrest. And in order to retain your attention for as long as possible, that one piece needs to make an impact. Artwork can be a great way of creating balance and capturing the eye as someone walks into the room.

Artwork can be a great way of creating balance and capturing the eye as someone walks into the room.

I'm often asked about my thoughts on feng shui; it is a complex practice that is studied with precision and passion, but the main principles are all about inviting good energy into your life and the lives of those around you, and I can't fault that. There are many principles of feng shui that I find fall under common sense, and I naturally follow these as good design practice. Other elements I don't agree with: sometimes it's just over-thought and sticking to them can end up hindering good design. While I'm certainly no master, I've got a good handle on the basics.

Feng shui means 'wind and water' and relates to your relationships and how you live within your environment. The principles are not only for your home but also for where you work, gardens and even where you might be buried. If feng shui is something you would like to investigate, I highly recommend reading up on it. Have a look at a few different books, not just one, as perceptions and interpretations differ.

Here are a few feng shui rules that I feel come under the common-sense banner; these are the principles I think add to the quality of your home and relationships. *Qi* means 'energy or life breath', and is a force said to be linked to prosperity.

FENG SHUI: *Front and back doors lining up causes qi to leak out, along with your good fortune.*
SB: If your front and back door line up, the wind will shoot through the house, slamming doors. You will feel the breeze going through your home, and this is quite unnerving. In feng shui they suggest putting an obstacle in the way; this is said to retain the *qi* for as long as possible and stop it from escaping too quickly. Putting something like a screen divider that moves out from the wall or an artwork on an easel can help deflect the wind force.

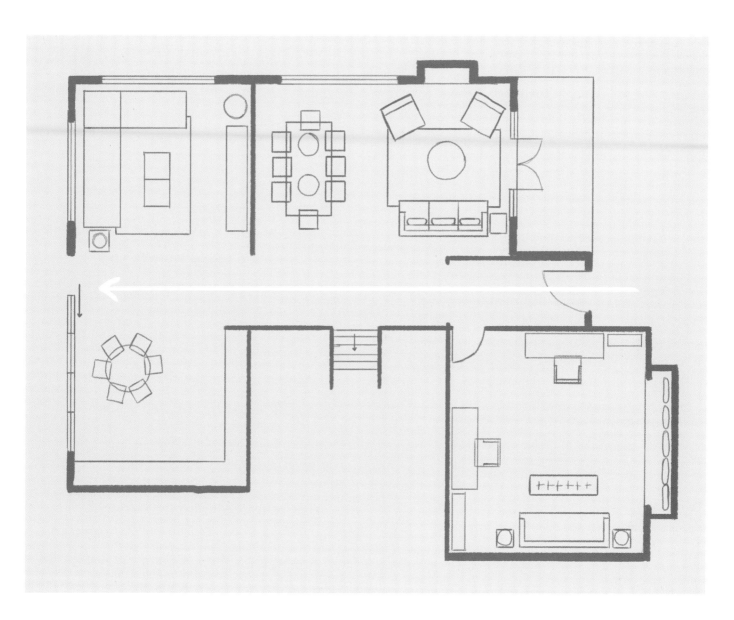

As for *qi* leaking out and taking your prosperity with it, think of the wind catching any papers you have sitting on a hall table and whipping them right out the door. If you are selling your house and have a 'wind tunnel' effect at your entry, people will be going out the door quick smart without giving an offer.

FENG SHUI: *The house is divided into different categories: business, public, heart and private.*
SB: There should be a demarcation of public and private spaces in your home, with the front door not opening directly into the kitchen, stairs,

toilet or bedroom. Now, in design if you have the stairs directly in line with the front door, it is considered confronting, in that it creates a physical block. Not only is the effect that people don't feel welcomed, I think it just heightens curiosity: straightaway your visitors are thinking, 'Hmmm, where does that lead?' More often than not the staircase will lead to the bedrooms upstairs, and that almost encourages people to poke around into your 'private' areas.

Having the staircase to the side, with a view of other rooms leading to the living areas diverts the eye after you notice the stairs. Having a strong paint colour or some dramatic artwork also helps take the focus off the stairs.

Quite a lot of bedrooms are right by the front door, and this is fine as long as the bedroom door doesn't line up with the front door. Leaving your door open at any time will mean that whoever comes into your house will get a great view of what's going on in the bedroom.

I remember a neighbour saying once that she missed having her bedroom by the front door: she loved keeping her door open so her beautiful bed linen was on display for everyone to see. So it really depends on who you're inviting into your home and what you want them to see. Personally, I prefer to keep my bedroom away from everyone's eyes: to me my bedroom is like a sanctuary, and a place I like to keep private.

Quite a lot of studies and formal areas sit at the front of the house. As these are deemed 'public' spaces within a house, this makes sense. No one wants their living room and kitchen on display every time the front door is opened. This would then leave you vulnerable to people looking in as they are walking by or else give a door-knocker an intimate view of how you live. Keeping your everyday areas hidden from the prying eyes of the outside world makes good sense.

If you live in an apartment, this can't always be avoided. But you can put up small screens, or sofa tables with lights, and this will create some sort of partition between the public and private spaces.

FENG SHUI: *Leaving your toilet door open and the toilet seat up loses you money.*
SB: Well, I don't know about money being lost other than it will give any potential buyer an icky feeling to see the toilet seat up. The last thing I want to see when I'm at someone's house is the toilet! I am amazed by the number of people who leave the door open and seat up. I have a little sign on our powder-room toilet door to 'Please close

door behind you.' To me, these feng shui points are not only common sense but common courtesy, so next time you are at someone's house close the toilet door!

> *Keeping your everyday areas hidden from the prying eyes of the outside world makes good sense.*

FENG SHUI: *A well-placed mirror will raise qi, make a space seem larger and magnify what they reflect.*
SB: Note the words 'well-placed'. A lot of people immediately think, 'Great, a mirror will add light and make the room larger so let's just whack one up here.' A mirror placed in haste could leave it reflecting a window, which sounds like the perfect solution if your home is dark and dingy, but think first about what is outside that window. A rubbish bin, people walking by or a car park is hardly going to add to the décor of your home, and if a mirror reflects a blank wall, all you are getting are two blank walls in your room.

Think of what the mirror will be reflecting and work out if it will enhance the space. If it won't, alter what the mirror is reflecting or move the position of the mirror till you are happy with what you see. I love to hang a mirror in a way that reflects artwork on the other side of the room. That way you get two bites of the cherry for the price of one artwork, and it adds instant colour without being too dominating: when you move around the room the view from the mirror will change.

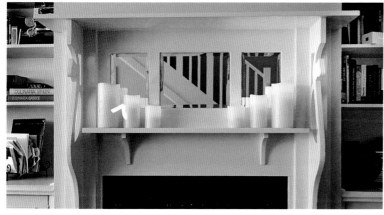

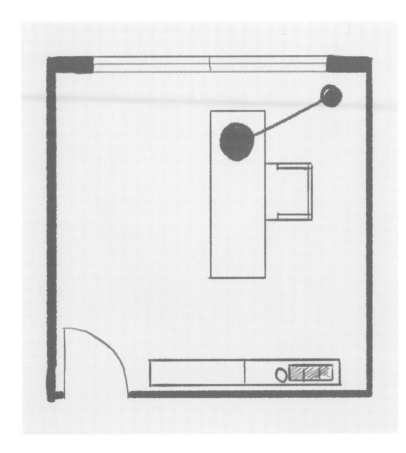

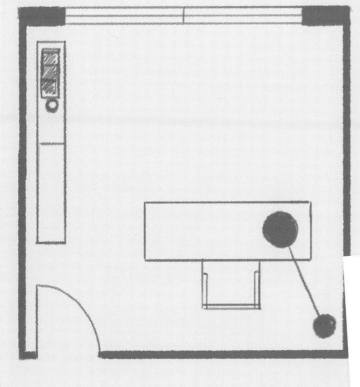

WORKSPACE: *Never have your back to the door so as not to see your enemies approaching.*

SB: Possibly a good point in an open-office environment; there's always a fair bit of backstabbing going on there. I don't know about you, but when I am working and engrossed in what I'm doing, if anyone walks into the room and I don't realise it, it can scare the bejeezus out of me! So, I agree, having your back to the door isn't the ideal layout at an office or in your home.

Having your desk against any of the other three walls or in the centre of the room is perfect, but what if you can't? If your desk has to be opposite the door, put the chair to the side so you can see movement in your peripheral vision. That way you won't be so jumpy when someone comes in to bring you a cup of tea. Or be really crafty and put a bucket of flour over the top of the doorway. *Then* no one will bother you!

The aim of feng shui principles is to improve how you live in an everyday sense. If there are certain elements in terms of layout or structure that don't feel right, trust your instincts and change them. This isn't a practice that will mean disaster if you don't follow it to the letter, but more about giving you simple tools to add flow and energy to your home. But, if you think it looks bad, then it probably does.

Having the desk facing the window not only means you have a great office view, but means you don't get glare on your computer screen.

KITCHEN
Where the feast begins and never ends

KITCHEN

To understand what you want in a kitchen, we need to go back to the basics of layout and function. The style of kitchens has changed dramatically in the past fifty years but what we actually do in that space has changed even more. Now, I might sound a bit like a school teacher at the beginning of this chapter, but you'll see how just a few simple tips can make a huge difference in getting the most out of your kitchen.

First, let's look at the nuts and bolts of a kitchen: the most common layout designs.

LAYOUT

GALLEY

Back when kitchens were hidden away from the rest of the house, this used to be one of the most common layouts. The galley kitchen simply comprises two adjacent walls with overhead cabinets on both sides. These kitchens are great for tight spaces but don't tend to be seen in modern homes, where more space is allowed. An adaptation of this style is where the kitchen is on only one wall of a room, facing outwards. Most often a nearby dining table is used for extra bench space, but these aren't deemed part of the kitchen layout. Galley kitchens can often be seen in apartments.

Every kitchen will have its point of difference in terms of how it runs, and in thinking carefully about what this is, your own unique space will evolve.

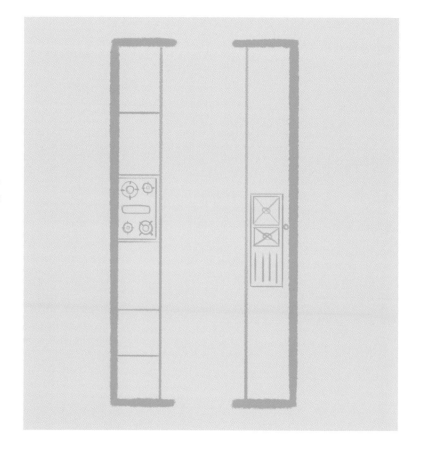

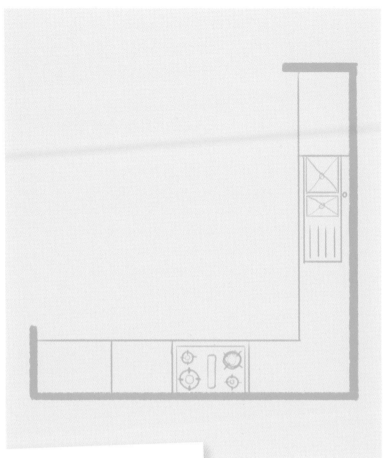

This leaves room to put in a dining table, not only for eating but as extra preparation space.

L-SHAPE

This one is pretty self-explanatory: an L-shape lay-out sees the working bench and appliance bench at a right angle. Once again, this style is commonly found in apartment-style living as it gives a small space an open feel.

U-SHAPE

This is a layout in a square or rectangular shape, and is very popular in big houses. The traditional U-shape does not have a second broken area for people to walk through. All traffic comes in and out the same direction.

ISLAND

Open-plan design loves an island bench. The bench can house the sink or the cooktop; it can have a one-plane surface or a raised secondary servery, which hides the workings and mess of the kitchen.

Whether you have a galley, L- or U-shaped kitchen, as soon as you put an island bench in there, that is what it is: an island bench kitchen. If you look at homes that have been recently built or renovated, in the majority of them you'll see a kitchen with an island bench.

FUNCTION

The very first noted principles of kitchen design were all about function, as evidenced by the once-popular phrase 'the working triangle'. This term was coined in the 1940s by the University of Illinois School of Architecture as part of its objective to create common standards in new builds. The three points of the triangle represent the main 'stations' of a typical kitchen: the fridge, the stove/oven and the sink. Of course, this was all conceived in the era when there was usually only one person in the kitchen – the housewife.

Each working area was supposed to be no less than 1200 mm wide and 2700 mm long. Now, nearly 3 m from one end of the 'triangle' to the other is a lot of distance to cover even if all you're doing is getting an egg from the fridge, filling the pot with water and putting it on the stove to boil. The basis of the triangle does still work but recently it has had a bit of a shake-up. With our vast number of modern cooking appliances and the ways we treat our kitchens today, the triangle now has more points than a hedgehog.

You don't need to be told the right shape for your kitchen by some fusty old academic types from a design school. You decide that. This is a decision that can only be made by you during the process of designing your dream kitchen.

Our kitchens have evolved alongside changes in our lifestyles: we've tended to favour open-plan living, with the kitchen no longer hidden away but sitting at the centre of things, a place from which we engage with family and friends. There's no more keeping the 'little woman' chained to the stove as she miraculously whips up a five-course dinner party menu, only appearing when it comes time to serve it. We're now more likely to be able to keep chatting to guests all the way through the cooking process.

That said, our love of convenience appliances has created a challenge to not only make our kitchen function well, but also make it look streamlined and not overly cluttered.

Every kitchen will have its point of difference in terms of how it runs, and in thinking carefully about what this is, your own unique space will evolve. Getting the right splashback or deciding which colour to feature should be far from your thoughts at this early stage, so put away the colour charts and pretty pictures and let's get serious about your kitchen's design.

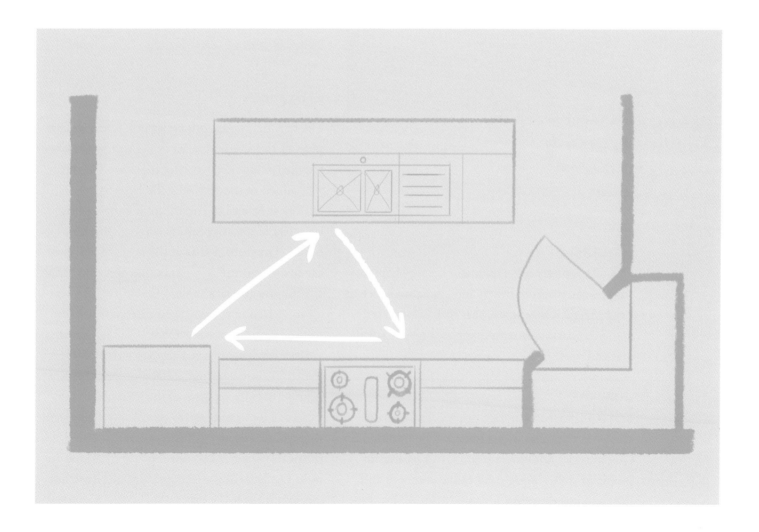

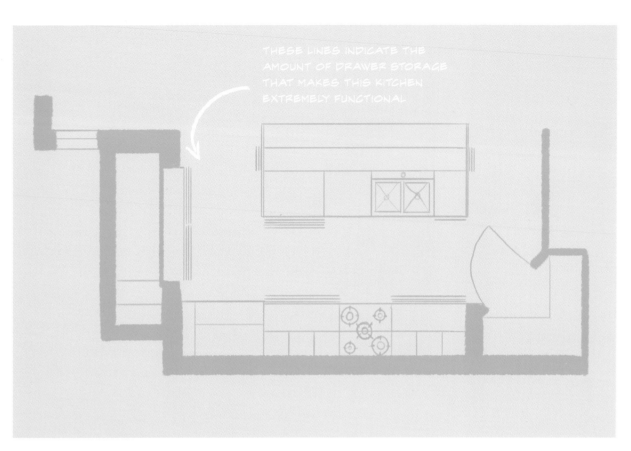

THESE LINES INDICATE THE
AMOUNT OF DRAWER STORAGE
THAT MAKES THIS KITCHEN
EXTREMELY FUNCTIONAL

It takes precision planning to
keep this a clutter-free kitchen.

WHERE TO START

A great way to get started is to do a simple itemised list of everything you use/do in your kitchen, and then rate the most-used appliances or actions. You may find the top three appliances are used just as much as the others and that's fine, but it must be a complete list. A great way to approach the task is to think about what you do first in the morning, and continue on throughout the entire day.

This process is less about de-cluttering than it is about prioritising.

Here is my example:

First thing, I put on the kettle, go to the pantry for my tea, as well as my breakfast food and vitamins, fill up a glass of water to wash down the vitamins, and then check the fridge for what I need to get ready for lunch or dinner that night.

At dinner-time, I defrost in the microwave, cook (sometimes using the oven but mostly the cooktop).

After dinner, I stack up all the dishes, put on the dishwasher, and that is the end of the day.

It doesn't sound like much, but break down these simple actions into point form and it becomes a long list.

- kettle
- sink
- pantry
- cooktop
- microwave
- freezer
- bin

My son would add to this:
- toaster

And for my husband:
- blender (used daily)

During the rest of the week, I would add:
- oven
- griller

Everything else in our kitchen, we use on an occasional basis.

Now, after you have completed the list of appliances, add the 'tools' that go with them.

For instance, in terms of my cooking, I have three pans I use regularly. I used to keep them in one of two oversized drawers that I had to fish through every day just to retrieve those three items.

On the other hand, I had history's smallest, untidiest, cutlery drawer; it was full of items I used constantly and yet could never find. There was a total imbalance between how my kitchen ran and how I cooked.

This process is less about de-cluttering than it is about prioritising. Your everyday items might include the coffee maker, the oven and the juicer, and these appliances will all form part of your working formula that will create the best functioning kitchen for you.

So rather than thinking, 'I want a massive oven because I see it in all the magazines and it looks really cool,' or, 'I want a matching red kettle and toaster because that's my favourite colour,' this is your opportunity to work out how *you* (or whoever is the cook at your place) like to cook and what the most important functions are in relation to that.

Each appliance on your list has an action and I want you to write down *what*, *how* and *where*, and finally the *outcome*.

A great example can be found in the humble bin. A rubbish bin used to be a simple thing, but now we have so many ways to store, recycle and discard that the right sort of bin can be a moral necessity. Don't answer with what you think you should say, but by considering how you work now and want to work in the future.

This can be a slow process, I know, but it ultimately helps to determine what you really want and need. Once you have gone through the '*what*, *how*, *where*, *outcome*' process, you can look at what is available in the marketplace that will suit your needs.

In this case, you might be amazed by how excited you can get about a bin! There are built-in versions, with containers of differing sizes, bins that slide out like drawers, others that appear when you open the door and bins that look like you've had a candy store installed in your kitchen.

Similarly, asking the right questions when picking a new oven will really help. What you want is the oven that will best suit your needs, not what is in fashion.

Having sections in your cutlery and utensil drawers creates efficiency in the kitchen.

COOKING

I *love* big freestanding ovens, but for me this is based on their look alone – I don't bake! (I can tell you, though, this came as a highly disappointing realisation, as I was really in 'I want, I want, I want' mode when I was considering my kitchen options). My mum would have loved one of these, as she was always baking Christmas cakes, wedding cakes and every biscuit and slice you could imagine. It would have taken pride of place in her kitchen and she would have used it every day.

In considering what type of oven you want, look at the different types of cooking that can be done with it. There are ovens that are oven–microwave combinations, and then there are steamer ovens. It is not uncommon to have a steamer oven and a separate convection–microwave combination, which essentially gives you two ovens. Keep in mind, though, that these come with certain height and width specifications. Look into this carefully, as you might find yourself with hardly any room left for bench space.

As well as the different types of cooking they do, ovens range quite dramatically in size from 600–700 mm to 900–1000mm. Make sure you choose an oven that will enhance your cooking, not overwhelm the kitchen.

It's important to get the most out of your oven not only in terms of what you cook but also the *way* you like to cook. There is fierce debate on whether a wall oven or under-bench oven is best. I think it just comes down to personal taste. Some argue that under-bench ovens can hurt your back, as you're constantly bending down to get the food out. This is a significant point not only for those with back issues but for those designing a kitchen for their 'forever' house, one they plan to live in till their eighties and beyond. Conversely, there is the argument that a wall oven in a small kitchen will take up valuable bench and storage space.

COOKTOPS

Gas cooking gets results quickly and is almost universally loved. On the other hand, induction cooking can really make people nervous. There's a belief out there that this is like the old 'element' cooking, meaning it takes you forever to cook on it, has a tendency to burn things as it is harder to control the temperature, and that the surface will burn your hand because it stays hot for too long after you've turned it off. These are, of course, all myths: the new technology of induction cooking does the total opposite of the old element cooking: you have similar temperature control to gas cooking. Induction cooktops are also very energy-efficient as they instantly boil and turn off, reducing heating times.

Look at the types of foods you cook on the stove, and how you like to cook them; do you stir fry, shallow or deep fry, sear, steam or simmer foods most often? Thinking about this will help

Select your oven to suit how you cook, not how you want it to look!

Induction cooktops give a streamlined look and are also very energy-efficient.

you to decide which type of cooktop will suit you best. If you are thinking of changing the type of cooktop you use, I recommend that you go into showrooms that hold cooking demonstrations so you can get a real feel for how the cooktop you have in mind works.

When it came to choosing my new oven, the focus was on the cooktop: I do 80 per cent of my cooking on it. But just because I use it for most of my cooking that didn't mean I had to get the most massive one out there! The big 900-mm cookers commonly come fitted with a wok burner and fish cooker. Now, this idea sounded good to me, until I gave it more thought: the heat of a wok burner is too intense for my type of cooking and I prefer to cook my fish in the oven. So, ultimately, I decided against a large cooktop: I didn't need all those bells and whistles, and it would have taken up too much valuable bench space.

Hidden range hoods give a sleek line to cabinetry.

TIP: When changing cooktops and/or ovens, check the amp requirements to see if your switchboard will be able to handle the load. It is common for an oven to have to go back to the shop after its new owner discovers it is going to cost $3000 to upgrade the switchboard.

HEAT EXTRACTORS

The most common types of range hoods are the big, bold canopies and the more discreet slide-out versions. Think about whether you are looking to make a statement in your kitchen through your choice of range hood, or whether you prefer to have it tucked away and sleek. They perform the same function, so apart from aesthetic consider-ations, it's a matter of looking at the size of the motor best suited to your preferred type of cook-ing. If you do a lot of frying and cooking of meat, you are going to want a pretty powerful range hood to accommodate all the hard work you will be putting your cooktop through.

Listen to working range hoods in showrooms as some can sound like small planes taking off.

If you want to put your cooktop on the island bench, there are some great ways to have a slick-looking kitchen, avoiding the traditional bulky canopy range hood. Vents called 'downdraft extractors' can be fitted either side of the cooktop, instantly dragging the smoke and aromas away from the room.

A stylish option in your island bench is using overhead vents that look like crystal lights. These are perfect if you live in a double-storey house or in an apartment, where venting isn't easy to achieve in a renovation. These vents are fitted with charcoal filters that process and break down fats, rather than having venting that needs to

Sexy and functional.

Downdraft extractors take away the need for overhead cabinetry.

duct into a cavity or an outside wall. You have to change the filters regularly but it is a small price to pay for such a sexy device.

BENCH SPACE

Most meal preparation is done around the sink and on the benches either side of it. Think about how you use your stove and bin, as well as the amount of bench space you need. If you have the tiniest space in the world and really need the extra bench space, this is where knowing some tricks can help. A sink can use up valuable bench space, but there are accessories that can help you make the most of a space-challenged kitchen.

You can look at fitting a sliding shelf that can 'pop out' to provide extra space. If you are really pressed for space, you can always put a chopping board on top of an open drawer. Don't forget,

though, that the runners won't take heavy items or the weight that comes with chopping.

Good kitchen preparation means having things within arm's reach. Cooking utensils should be right next to the stove. Having them tucked away in a drawer will give your kitchen a sleek appearance, but keeping them in a jar serves just as well. You can even put the jar away at the end of cooking to keep that clean look without bearing the cost of fitting an extra drawer.

Fitting trays right next to the stove makes good use of a small area, and stacking them vertically saves you from having to constantly rattle around in the bottom of a drawer looking for them.

Spices and condiments can be kept in a slide-out drawer next to the oven or you can make use of the (minimal but still useable) space at the front of the range hood.

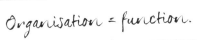

Organisation = function.

TIP: If you are keen on fitting a cooktop in your island bench, this is best looked at around the time of building, as there are certain allowances that need to be made for this type of layout.

WASHING UP

Our sinks have undergone a bit of a revolution – from a single bowl with a drainer to a double bowl and drainer, and then on to under-bench and over-bench variations… and I'm sure by the time you've finished reading this sentence there will be three more versions available. If you love using your dishwasher, you probably won't need the double sink. But if you have an open kitchen, the double-bowl sink can be a good place to stash items from the bench when guests drop around unexpectedly.

When planning a new kitchen, it's highly likely you'll be including a dishwasher. Even if you don't use one, to try to sell a house without a dishwasher is almost unheard of, and could be a negotiating tool for a buyer to bring your price down.

Selecting a dishwasher is simple, with the options being a one door or two-drawer action, and either a solid face or integrated version. A solid face is your standard dishwasher that usually comes in white or stainless steel. An integrated dishwasher gives you the option of putting a face on the front that matches your cabinets. Some integrated dishwashers have their buttons on the inside of the face or even a fancy remote to get the action started. An integrated face hides the dishwasher and gives a kitchen a very sleek look.

A double-drawer dishwasher is perfect for apartments, as well as for small, growing or 'empty nest' families. Even though we are a family of four, we hardly ever used our old dishwasher: it was rare for us all to be there at the same time and so it was difficult to justify putting on a full load. It was time to get a new dishwasher, and a two-drawer version was the perfect option for us.

A busy household will need a full dishwasher, but your kitchen is a permanent fixture, so make sure you're thinking ahead to the future needs of your family. For example, if you have teenagers, consider what you'll need in a couple of years' time when the kids have their licences and will be out of the house most of the time.

Remember when we talked about the kitchen's 'working triangle' and ways of making a kitchen efficient? Well, looking at how you empty your dishwasher can be one of the best ways to judge how efficiently your space is working.

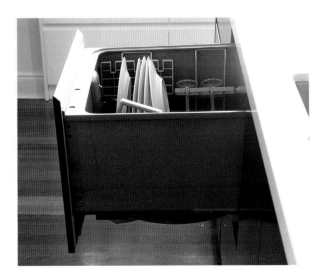
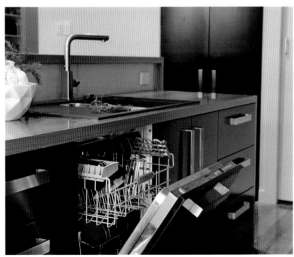

BIN

We all need somewhere to get rid of the crap in the kitchen. But these days, discarding waste is not quite as simple. We need to separate out the recycling and I also like to do some composting of organic waste.

It makes sense to have all these waste receptacles in one place, preferably within easy reach of both the prep bench for when you're getting meals ready, and the sink for when you're washing up. I always try to incorporate bins into the cupboard space so I can open a door or drawer, all my bins are in the one spot, and I can close the door on them when I'm done.

APPLIANCES

The invention of the appliance cupboard meant our whole world wasn't on show to anyone who dropped around. The appliances our family uses a number of times during the day, such as the kettle, tend to be left on the kitchen bench full time, but the rest – toaster, blender, sandwich maker, coffee grinder, popcorn maker, juicer, handheld blender . . . yes, we really do have a lot! – we keep hidden away. That said, the cycle of moving them up to the bench and hiding them away again can be exhausting, not to mention make keeping the kitchen clean a tedious task.

As appliances are relatively cheap and highly subject to fads, we all tend to collect them like orphaned puppies. In the end, they just take up valuable space and their mere presence can cause you grief and stir up buyer's remorse: you were sure you were going to use that jam maker more than three times.

This is an area of the kitchen where I recommend de-cluttering, as the appliance cupboard too easily becomes a home for the 'that will come in handy one day' gadgets. Be realistic and get rid of the appliances you know you don't – and won't – use.

Once you're left with the appliances that actually make life easier, there are quite a few clever ways you can create a hidden storage area for your appliances. One is creating a cabinet on the benchtop with a roll-top cupboard at bench height. Another is to go the whole way and put in full-height doors.

STORAGE

You can integrate your appliance storage space within the pantry, but just make sure there is enough airflow. You don't want moisture building up in the same place you store food.

Finally we get to the best part: eating! One of my favourite sayings has to be, 'You'll always find me in the kitchen at parties' – a saying so good, a song was even written about it. Our kitchens are the beating heart of our homes and once you have worked hard to get your kitchen right, it is all about chilling out, spending time with people, and eating well. Just have a think about all the different types of eating you do in your kitchen:

- in front of the fridge
- in front of the pantry (I thought I would get these two out the way first, in case you were feeling guilty)
- at the bench
- snacks after school
- snacks at dinner parties, while you are getting the main course ready
- lunch
- dinner, if you can't be bothered moving to another area.

The way people eat these days tends to be casual and informal, and sitting at the kitchen bench is one of the most popular spots to nosh. Along with allowing for our serving and preparation needs, the amount of bench space in our kitchens should accommodate how we eat and where we like to do it.

If eating at the bench is likely to be popular at your place, and you are putting in or updating a centre island bench, make sure it is 1000–1200 mm deep. This will mean there's enough room for someone to be seated on one side while someone else works or puts out plates on the other.

The biggest obstacle in terms of bench space is the kitchen sink. We are used to having everything symmetrical, and naturally the sink ends up in the middle. This isn't always the most practical position. Try putting the sink to one side to give a more useable amount of bench space in one area.

If you have more than two cooks in the family who love being in the kitchen together, try having two sinks. One can be allocated to dishes and the bulky cleaning up, and the other, a smaller one, used for things like preparing food and rinsing glasses. This will keep the clutter on the bench to a minimum as you won't be keeping all the dishes stacked up on the bench while you are cooking.

If you don't have the room but still want an island bench, get a butcher's block on wheels that you can move around as extra bench space. This can become the place for part of the preparation or be used to stack plates, keeping the main bench free for entertaining.

BEFORE AND AFTER - CASE STUDY

BEFORE: This kitchen may have ticked the boxes in the traditional working triangle but lacked efficiency in regards to how things were stored. Clean dishes were constantly in the dishwasher and sink as putting them away meant countless trips up and down the length of the kitchen.

Here, the dishwasher was at one end of the kitchen, and the plates and cups were kept in two different places at the other.

AFTER: By moving the dishwasher to the other end of the kitchen and changing the storage area for bowls and plates, emptying the dishwasher can now be done in one to two footsteps. This is a very simple solution to making a boring task more efficient.

Not only is the kitchen the heart of the home at meal times, it is often where everyone gathers before and after school and work. It becomes a makeshift office, a place to keep an eye on the kids while they're doing their homework, as well as a dumping ground for mail, keys, toys and anything else that doesn't have another place to live.

Every kitchen needs a 'go-to' drawer or cupboard. There are things that always need to be at hand to all members of the family at any one time, such as batteries, sticky tape and rubber bands. You could have all these things stored somewhere in the office, pantry or laundry, but if you have a go-to drawer right at the centre of the action, it means you won't be the one always having to rush around trying to find the spare batteries for the remote. You'll just have to train the rest of the family to top it up when things are used (good luck!).

This drawer or cupboard can also house a tray or basket that sits on the bench during the day. All the household's random 'stuff' can go in there instead of the five different places they are normally left on the kitchen bench. If people come over and you want to hide it, whisk it away back into the drawer/cupboard.

Most of the ideas here sound as though they are about designing your kitchen from scratch, but there are many suggestions you can use even if you're just tweaking your layout. A few simple changes can make an instant difference to your kitchen and its functionality.

Look at your cabinets, for instance: most only have one shelf inside – such a big waste of space. Standard base cabinets come in 400 mm, 600 mm or 900 mm widths, and you can easily turn a 600–900 mm two-door cabinet into a set of drawers.

By getting a cabinet-maker to convert that space into drawers for your cups and plates gives you greater access to the whole depth of the area.

Most of the time we only use what is at the front of fixed shelves as it is too hard to access everything sitting right up the back.

Another quick fix can be to purchase a new bench top with added width. This will dramatically increase the size of your island bench, and make it a better more useable space for meals and homework. You won't even need to change the cabinets underneath, just add a little extra support with either upright legs or a thicker substrate underneath the new benchtop. This is a task I would get a professional in to do as the weight and size of the new bench needs to be taken into consideration.

TIP: If you'd like to update your kitchen, but want to focus your spend on the fittings and surfaces, keep all the plumbing and the oven in the same positions. This will keep labour costs down.

Your kitchen is one of the most used rooms in the house so take the time to write your lists and think through all the functions and appliances you use. Don't get hung up on the idea that the 'dream' can't be a reality. Even if your new kitchen isn't happening today, you'll be creating great plans to work towards for the future.

Moving the sink to an off-centre position opens up a single-bench area. Instead of having a medium amount of space on each side, this bench has ample room to prep and serve dinner at the same time.

The larger sink at the rear bench keeps all the big items away from the main prep area in the island bench.

RULES ROUND-UP

- Work out your daily tasks to make your kitchen as efficient as possible.

- List your favourite and most often cooked meals to work out the appliances that suit you.

- Do an inventory of freestanding appliances you use often for the right storage options.

- Determine which storage areas you can double up on – for example, cups with tea and coffee.

- Drawers are a better use of space than deep-set cupboards.

- Have cooking utensils and condiments in drawers and on shelves next to or above the cooking centre.

- Have your everyday plates, bowls and cutlery within arm's reach of the sink and dishwasher for efficient clean-up.

DINING &
ENTERTAINING

Dine by design

DINING & ENTERTAINING

Our family has the normal places we eat – sitting at the kitchen bench and in a formal dining area – but we also eat in almost all the other rooms of the house. There are strawberries and champagne in the bath, breakfast (and crumbs) in bed or on the patio, barbecues outdoors, pizza on our laps in front of the TV, and casual chips and dips with friends in the living room, with a glass of wine in hand.

There are so many considerations when you think about food and drink in the home. I often hear people say there is no need for a separate formal dining area any more; the kitchen is where we usually dine these days. With technology and computer screens taking over work and home entertainment, and the rush of busy schedules for work, sport and part-time jobs, the art of conver-

sation over dinner will soon become a quaint old anecdote that'll make kids roll their eyes.

'We used to sit at the table with the family every night of the week to talk about our day.'

'Talking to someone over a table? What is that?'

You don't need a formal room for a family discussion but you do need a delegated space to communicate with everyone in the house as a unit. Food evokes passion and love, and sharing a meal is an important ritual that should be happening on a regular basis. Whatever space you have in your home, pizza on the lap in front of the telly should be limited to once a week. Even if it means having to get a fold-up table and chair set, this, to me, is one of the most important elements that completes a home.

Whether sitting at the table or the bench, food is about bringing families together.

KITCHEN

AT THE BENCH

The kitchen bench has become one of the most important congregational areas of the home, especially with our lifestyles leaning towards more casual living rather than formal dining. As we discussed in the kitchen chapter, getting the depth measurements right for the bench is essential if you have seating next to it. This will give the right depth for the person in the kitchen to still cook or do the prep while someone can sit and eat opposite them, without getting in the way of the cooking.

Just because you have a bench out in the open, that doesn't mean you'll have stools there too. If your dining/kitchen table is right next to the bench, it might become a case of a 'battle of the seats'. If your kitchen bench and table are only a metre apart, keep the space for your dining chairs and a clear pathway. You can still stand comfort-ably at the bench with a wine in your hand, chat to the chef and nibble away, knowing you have the comfort of a dining chair to fall back on. If, however, you have a couple of small kids who you'd like to have sit at the bench at breakfast times or keep an eye on while you're cooking, you can have two stools only, which slide under the bench and to one side, out of the way of the dining chairs. Or else you can have a booster on a dining chair that can be shifted to the kitchen bench when needed.

For good leg-room space at the kitchen bench, stick to a minimum of 250 mm under the counter. This gives enough room to slide the chair under, as well as room for your legs when sitting at the bench.

The benefit of having a deep bench (say, 1200 mm deep) is the space underneath that can be kept for extra storage. This might be just for excess items that you don't access every day, but never, ever leave a useful space empty in a kitchen!

As great as it is having everyone congregate around the kitchen bench, the kicking of the under-counter by those sitting on stools is always a big problem. You can't stop people doing this: dangling legs won't be able to help themselves pushing against the wall for stability. So, make sure you don't have high-gloss or painted surfaces that will mark easily. Having stools with footrests will help.

AT THE TABLE

This is where the rest of the action happens. Our kitchen tables are not only a place to eat but a place to do school projects, run the home office, not to mention end up as a veritable dumping ground. Any surface is fair game for a mess. To combat the office and school-project issues, have a look in the home office chapter: there I talk about storage and hide-away solutions that will help with the excess clutter life throws at you.

The kitchen table is perfect for spreading things out on, but at dinner-time it should be able to be cleared quickly. If you reserve the kitchen table as a project table and not an eating space, there goes your easiest and quickest way to communicate as a family or couple.

The kitchen table can be a long statement piece or petite and nondescript. The position of the table in the room will determine the shape, size and whether you invest good money into it as a feature.

My formal dining table takes the same battering as the casual kitchen table and tends to be an even more popular dumping ground, as it isn't used regularly. More often than not, the formal dining table will be more of a feature, with surfaces that make it stand out from the casual dining table in a home.

Trawling the shops looking for that perfectly grained timber top or the right set of legs are the last things you should do in selecting your table. I have had many clients put amazing tables on eBay because they took over the space and became big 'lumps' that no one could move around, and all because it was bought for that one Christmas dinner a year. Whether you prefer casual or formal dining, these are similar considerations when planning and selecting a table.

TABLE SIZE

This is governed by how many people live in your house, how often extra people sit at your table and the size of your space.

Here I use a family of four as an example. There's Mum, Dad, two kids, and at weekends or during the week the odd friend joins them. At the weekend the extended family might drop in and stay for a casual dinner, or impromptu drinks and nibbles might happen with a barbecue starting up outside. Mother's Day and Christmas is a formal sit-down dinner, and occasionally they'll host a

group of friends for a 'grown-up' sit-down dinner. There is only one place to eat with no formal dining room but there is an outdoor area. So how do you accommodate this big variation in seating and styles of dining?

To seat eight people at a table you need the length to be 2400 mm x 900–1000 mm deep.

The most common table size, 1800 mm x 800 mm, will comfortably sit six chairs. A chair needs an allocated space of 500 mm with a minimum of 100 mm either side. If you change that to bench seats on the sides, you can fit three people on each side and two chairs on the end.

Grab two kitchen stools and you can now fit ten people for a casual get-together where no one expects any airs and graces.

You can dress the same table for a formal dinner for six.

Now for the big family gatherings. When you come to buy an outside table, look for one the same size and width as your general dining table or store a large trestle table that you can fit in the living area. You can either use linen to make it look like one large space or use a long table runner to give it a dressed look without going too formal.

Flexibility is the key when you only have one dining space to work with.

A round table also gives you flexibility: you can keep adding chairs in a very casual way, but of course it doesn't give you the ability to join on other tables. Round tables are perfect when you have a formal dining area as well.

TIP: A small bench or sofa table nearby is perfect for putting out the extras, like salad bowls and bottles of wine, to give you extra space on the table

---

To take the stark and stiff feel out of a formal room, a round table will always give a great conversational feel to your dinner party. Fabric chairs lend elegance to a setting and also keep your guests comfortable during the whole three courses, *and* maybe even help them to stick around for a few extra drinks afterwards.

A formal dinner party is about creating intimacy so pick the table size you'll be using on a regular basis. If you like holding big dinner parties, but only once a year, don't choose a twelve-seater as your permanent table. You can always hire a table for that one event. Keep your room attuned to what goes on daily.

Carver chairs take up extra room at a dining table and you need to allow a minimum of 800 mm for the chair and 200 mm either side for that luxurious dining experience.

If you love the look and feel of carvers but don't have the space, put them at the end of the table only. This will also give a stylish, formal look to your dining area.

A round table also gives you flexibility: you can keep adding chairs in a very casual way, but of course it doesn't give you the ability to join on other tables.

SURFACES

To coaster or not to coaster? There are ways to test the type of dining experience you want to create. The best one is whether your heart leaps every time a cup or plate touches a surface. If so, keep it a bit more formal. A formal dining table most probably goes with trimmings of placemats and coasters and larger mats for hot bowls and teapots and cups.

If you're a fan of the more casual experience, it means you probably won't bother with placemats and coasters on a day-to-day basis, but you'll still use them for special occasions and for hot items. No surface is impervious to stains and heat, so even if you want the most casual dining environment, if you don't take care certain things will mark your table. Sometimes that adds to the beauty and character of the surface and other times it can ruin a perfectly good finish of a table just out of carelessness.

TIP: Get your cabinet-maker to make a trivet/chopping board from the cut-off of your sink or cooktop. Put rubber stops underneath so it doesn't scratch the bench.

LIGHTING

Seeing what you are eating is reasonably important, so getting the balance between this and creating a mood is the key to a great dining experience.

The Showroom: SURFACES

These surfaces are used also in your kitchen benches and working surfaces so use this as a guide for the kitchen chapter.

MARBLE

This is a tough but porous surface that will have a seal on it, but you'll need to be careful of acidic liquids, such as red wine and lemon juice. When they are spilt wipe within the first hour to reduce the chance of staining. You can put hot cups and teapots directly onto it as well as some hot pans, but all marbles are different so I would get an off-cut to have as a trivet for your hot pans to test if it marks or leaves yellow scorchmarks. Otherwise, marble can be treated roughly, you can roll your pastry on it, use it as a chopping board and any wearing imperfections add to the character of the stone. The less sheen it has, the more loved it looks.

COMPOSITE STONE

This has many similar qualities to marble so needs the same care. It's a tough surface but can't be treated as roughly as marble, however, as it doesn't take on the same worn character from knife marks, and so on. Once again, ask for a cut-off to test the surface for any rough treatment before you experiment on an expensive top.

CONCRETE

A floated and polished concrete top is a stunning piece, but it is better suited to your kitchen bench or a fixed outdoor dining table. Trying to move this is not recommended either! It can be full of imperfections and flecks or smooth with a high-gloss finish. Concrete is a porous material and will be affected similarly to marble and natural stone. It can't be treated as a precious surface so expect wear and tear, marks and the rest.

LAMINATE

As with paintwork, the sheen of the laminate will determine the toughness of the surface. High gloss will be more vulnerable to scratching than a textured laminate. Do not chop or put hot things directly onto the surface as these marks cannot be repaired.

CORIAN

Not many tables are made with corian so this is more about the kitchen bench. The big benefit of this material is it can be moulded to make different shapes: a bench can be moulded to look like the sink is part of the bench with no seams. The added benefit is you can put hot things straight onto the surface and any scratches, burns or imperfections can be buffed out and fixed as you would a car panel.

TIMBER

From recycled to mirror-finish, there are so many different types of timber surfaces for your tables and benches. As in flooring there are different grades in timbers that take it from a soft to hard timber. If you love the natural wear and tear of timber and the way dints and rough treatment adds character, you can really look at any timber you want.

Have the surface finished in a matt or low sheen to give it that raw, natural look. High gloss and perfect surfaces tend to be for formal tables and this also means solid painted timber tops and not just stained wood. No timber is impervious to marks and stains, so even if you use hard woods like redgum, ironbark, jarrah, blackwood and oak, to name just a few, you still need to take care to keep the 'even' beauty of the timber. Most Australian hardwoods are perfect for dining tables, so look at the colours and varieties available to create a statement piece in your dining room.

The good thing about timber is it can be sanded, re-painted and stained at any time, but this isn't something you want to do often. Take care of you timber tabletops to ensure their longevity.

The Showroom: LIGHTING

DOWNLIGHTS

Downlights over a casual eating area are perfect to show off your gourmet cooking in a flood of light. More direct lighting, like a hanging pendant, creates atmosphere for your day-to-day meals.

STATEMENT LIGHTING

A statement chandelier is always going to grab attention. To make it work, you need to keep the table decorations simple and only use with low-lying flower arrangements and candles.

FLEXIBLE LIGHTING

A flexible lighting arrangement, like an arched floor lamp, means you can have it one way for everyday use and then swing it over for a more focused look, creating an intimate mood for your dinner party.

CANDLELIGHT

Candlelight can give any dining experience a wonderful ambience. Make sure you have other lighting available in the form of an up-light, table or floor light, as just using candles alone could leave you wondering what you are actually eating!

STYLING

You can turn the dullest table into a glamorous experience just by the way you dress it. From the china to the cutlery and glasses right up to the table settings, this is one of my favourite parts of dinner, and so I say, be creative! The way you dress your table adds a whole new dimension to how you dine.

A barbecue is all about the condiments, relaxing and enjoying the food, so don't feel you have to impress with centrepieces. Concentrate on the bowls your salads go in, the group of bottles and the glassware. Your plates can be paper or plastic and you can use cutlery or your fingers, it doesn't matter. Keep the decorations simple and the colours lively.

Day-to-day eating and sticking to the basics doesn't mean you need to be boring. A table runner in the centre adds colour and mood and also doubles as a coaster for drinks and the extras. Or use placemats that can become a feature of the table or kitchen bench.

A semi-formal dinner means still keeping it casual but showing attention to some details. I am a big fan of using your good tableware on a regular basis, not just for that one special dinner a year. Use flowers or candles as a centrepiece but keep it low-key rather creating than a big dramatic scheme.

The attention paid to your cutlery, chinaware and accessories, like mats and napkins, becomes a highlight in this dining experience. Get it right and people will sit differently, act differently and definitely eat differently. Keep the name place tags for weddings and birthdays with an '0' at the end of them, and make these dinners more personal. If you want flowers to be a feature, put them in a tall vase that is a focal point on the table at the beginning of the night, and then move them to a buffet when people sit down (so they can actually see each other).

For something different, incorporate the arrangement into the dinner: have some herbs subtly mixed in with the flowers and snip off when the food is served. The fragrance of the herbs will add to the aroma of your food. Stay away from scented candles as a strong perfumed smell can detract from the meal.

A gathering of a few girlfriends for formal high tea means it is all about the china and how the table is laid. Create a small buffet in a group of plates or in tiers at the centre or side of the table. To give a casual feel mismatch your cutlery but always have linen napkins. Hand-picked flowers and big pots of tea are essential, as is a sense of fun and elegance.

When all of these elements come together, your conversation will flow, and whether it's a tête-à-tête or a large dinner for twenty, it will be the most successful dinner party you ever had.

The placement and style of your chairs will be about comfort, and the right size table for the space will decide whether you feel overwhelmed or cramped. When all of these elements come together, your conversation will flow, and whether it's a tête-à-tête or a large dinner for twenty, it will be the most successful dinner party you ever had.

RULES ROUND-UP

- At the kitchen bench, choose stools that are the right height with foot rests for comfort and keeping busy feet still.

- Keep the conversation pit for family meals and not school projects. Make sure clutter is cleared away easily every night if it is the only table in the house.

- Make sure the table size and shape suits how you eat on an everyday basis, not just for that one special dinner at Christmas. Look at how your table can be flexible to accommodate an increasing number of guests.

- Use the coaster as your guide when choosing surfaces. Coaster = a surface that needs care and attention. No coaster = a surface that will mark, age and have 'character' over time.

- Have statement lighting and a dimmer to create different moods throughout the meal.

- A basic table can become a high-end restaurant with the right styling, but don't be too precious if you are just having a barbecue.

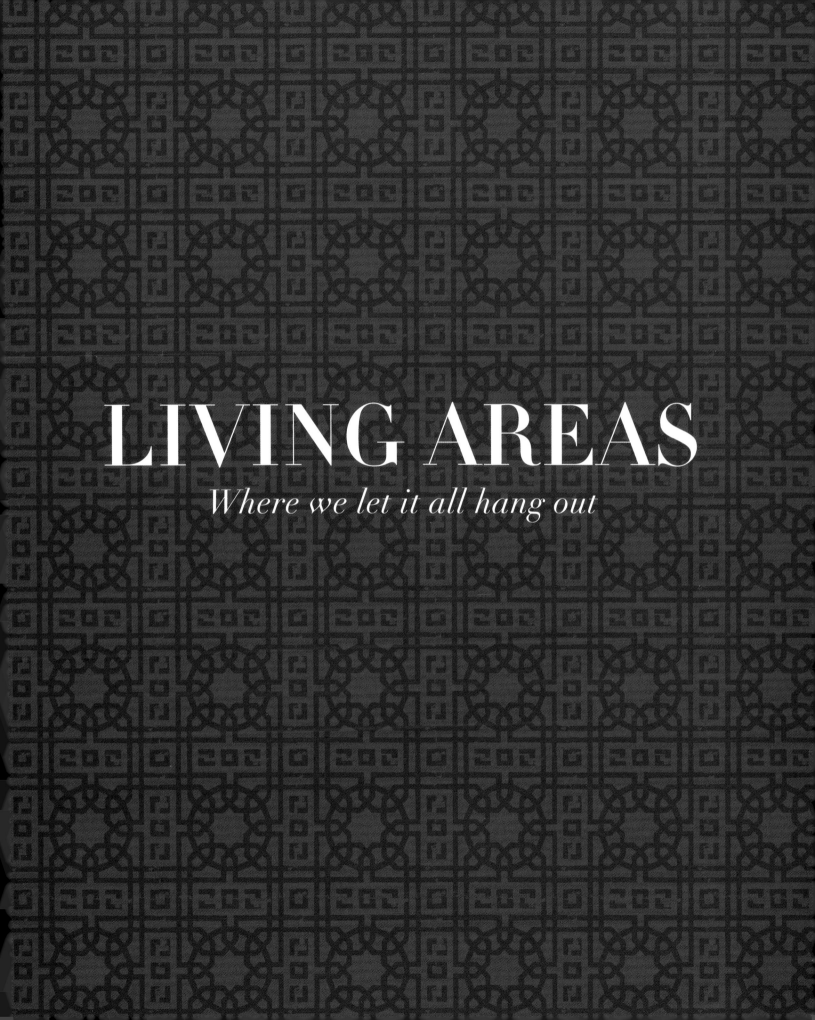

LIVING AREAS

Where we let it all hang out

LIVING AREAS

Our living spaces are where our lives are on display. Our front doors will often open up straight into our lounge rooms, or else it's only a short journey up the hallway before we come across the main living area. This is where your guests are immediately given a snapshot of your style: the colours you love, the décor you've chosen, your taste in art. It can also lead to snap judgements: you're a mad collector of Babushka dolls, you love clutter, you have a tendency towards OCD, you have no control over your life and have just plain given up trying.

Feeling exposed yet? Well, you should be. Everyone from the neighbours to tradies and the kids' friends, as well as your own family and friends will walk into your home and mentally take stock: 'Well, this is *you*'. This is never said out loud, and perhaps people won't even acknowledge that they're doing this, but there's no doubt about it: our living spaces reflect how we live as an individual and a family as well as the way we welcome people into our lives.

The formal room has increasingly lost favour in new builds, which concentrate more on outdoor spaces as the sites for family entertainment and gatherings. Coupled with this, our lives are more open plan than ever before. New houses rarely include a formal room, and in 80 per cent of renovations, a wall is knocked out to make one big living space, mostly incorporating the kitchen and dining areas.

When it comes to arranging furniture and fitting everything in, having one big room has to be easier to manage than a number of pokey little rooms, right? It sounds good in theory but more often than not, one big room creates one big problem! Where do you put all that furniture and how do you stop it from feeling like a barn house or a breezy causeway in an airport?

Our houses may have big rooms and lots of them, but we tend to cram all our social interaction into the living room. This means that sometimes these spaces get over-filled and out of control. On the other end of the scale, I've seen instances where clients have been un-sure about how to fill the room properly: there's a couch at each of far ends of the room and one person practically has to call the other to ask them if they'd like a drink or tell them to change the channel on the TV.

An exaggeration? Probably, but I'm sure there are quite a lot of you wondering how to make a large room feel more intimate and a small room seem larger. No matter what you do in these rooms – eating, entertaining, watching TV, hanging out – these are the two most common questions I hear when it comes to any main living area.

I know it sounds as though this can be dealt with in a page or two, but let me tell you: these two simple questions bring up a whole lot of other issues. But there is also a raft of practical solutions I will offer. I hope you are ready to face a few home truths about how you live in your living spaces.

Once upon a time our houses had both a 'good room' and a family room. Often, the good room was where you could wrest back a little bit of the control you'd lost in the rest of the house. It was the one place where everything had a spot and stayed there. The good room acted to soothe so much anxiety: 'The kids are the reason the rest of the house is a nightmare. This is where the real me resides. See? I *am* organised.'

Some of the formal rooms you might see today are on a par with museum displays; all that's miss-ing is a cardboard sign saying 'do not sit'. In fact, most of these sorts of rooms don't even need the sign: just by looking at the interior you know you will be rushed through to where the action really happens – the living space.

OPEN-PLAN LIVING

Open-plan living can pose a lot of obstacles to a clean, sophisticated-looking functional lounge-room layout, but it helps to think about the most common activities that take place in this space. Most people will answer 'watching TV and sitting on the couch'. And *voila*, these are your top priorities. If they're *not* your two priorities, this is half your luck. At my place, the 'conversation pit' is in another room in the house, and I tend to be there most often talking to myself!

THE TELEVISION

The TV is possibly one of the ugliest features in the house – although most men would disagree. Most modern homes and renovations put such an emphasis on creating full walls of windows that there is usually only one wall which a TV can sit against – if you are lucky, you might have a choice between two. Not so long ago we had TV cabinets that took up a huge footprint in the room because TVs were so deep. We all acknowledged they were ugly, which led to huge cabinets with fitted doors – an eyesore to fix another eyesore! So, I have to say, I'm pretty happy with how slim TVs are these days. They still aren't my favourite feature, but we have a lot more choice when it comes to decorating a room with them in it.

SIZE

How large your TV is will determine the size of your cabinet and how you decorate either side of it. A large TV needs to sit on a large cabinet to give it balance. Whether the TV is wall-mounted or sits on a cabinet, a minimum width of 300 mm either side of the TV is needed so that it doesn't overwhelm the space. You can go longer, or even extend

A cabinet like this was the main feature of the room.

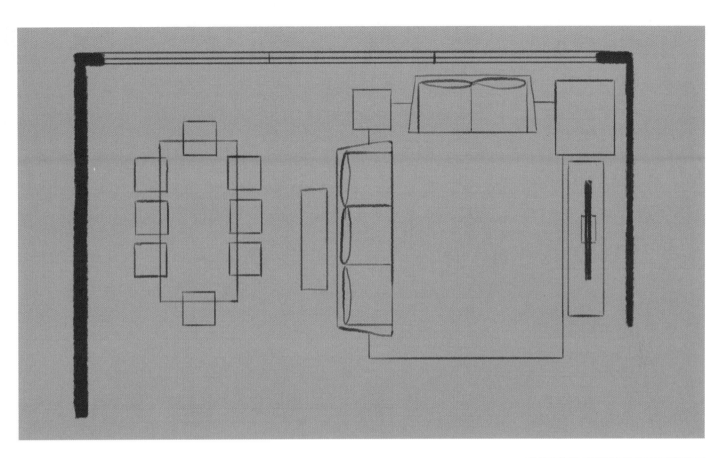

built-in cupboards and drawers across the entire length of the wall.

Decorating around the TV is one of the hardest things to do: you don't want to crowd the TV or make the area look cluttered by creating too many focal points on the one wall.

The key with the cabinets on the wall is that their height must balance with the length of the wall. With just a low-lying cabinet, the wall in the picture above would have seemed empty but using large pieces of artwork would have made it look too busy. These staggered slim-line cabinets give more of a sculptural feel, rather than simply looking like rows of storage boxes. The mixture of open and concealed storage means there's room for hiding away the basics, like DVDs, as well as leaving the shadow boxes for decorating flourishes.

A full wall of black is a dramatic touch, and perfect for an entertaining area. Painting the wall black has two benefits: when the TV isn't on, it almost disappears into the wall; and it creates an expansive feel so when the TV is on it's almost like being at a cinema. The floating shelves enhance the dramatic effect, and the LED lights create shadows, giving texture to the flat wall.

Hidden lights behind the panelling create a dramatic backdrop.

Hidden storage is the key to reducing visual clutter.

An ottoman is the perfect place to hide any extras that aren't used every day, such as TV guides, magazines and the extra remotes.

Make sure your DVDs and accessories fit within the measurements of the drawers.

TV ACCESSORIES

With TVs come all the other entertainment 'boxes', such as cable, hard-disk recorders, gaming consoles and their accessories, surround-sound systems and DVD/CD players. Storage is often compromised in order to achieve a streamlined look, but a room filled with clutter is going to completely detract from this. Look for storage everywhere you can: in your cabinetry, overhead and even in your seating.

I think over the years I have only had a single client who has managed to program all their remotes into one. Most households are wrangling a minimum of three, and I've seen places with up to six or seven! Trays are your friend in any living space: have a couple of sizes of trays to work with the remotes, TV guides and the drinks and food that go with your entertainment. You can look at a 'three step' of trays, where they sit inside each other, or else have a number of different ones with each one serving a distinct purpose.

Now, I guarantee the remotes won't always be in their place whenever you walk back into the room, but I find the trays become like a 'homing pigeon' base for your remotes, and over time are less likely to be found under the couch, pushed between the cushions or left on the kitchen bench.

DECORATIVE TRAYS

Trays that match the décor in your room mean you have a functional and decorative piece.

TRAY SETS

Sets of trays mean you can have them all in the one spot, with the smallest for the remotes, and the larger ones coming out to play when the day's activity turns into a group session.

SIDE TABLE TRAYS

Having trays on your side tables also protects the furniture while still being decorative.

FURNITURE

The types of furniture in your living space will be determined by a few factors: how you like to sit, how many people live in your home, and how many extra people come around on a weekly basis.

Here's an example: a family of four love to watch the TV together, shoes off, curled up and lounging. The perfect layout for them is a corner suite with a 900–1000 mm-depth couch.

The distance between the lounge (or wherever you watch TV from) and a widescreen TV needs to be a minimum of 2 metres. Depending on the size of your screen, you'll need to adjust the distance between it and your main seating area. Most guides recommend the distance between the pair be two and a half times the size of your TV. So,

if you have one of the popular 42-inch (106-cm) screens, you'll need to sit just over 2.5 m away. This, of course, is just a guide and the calculations will vary depending on the quality of your TV, whether it is LCD or plasma, and the quality of the pixilation.

To make this formula work for you, start with the minimum requirement, then when your TV is in place you can work out if you need it slightly further away or closer. These kinds of rules work well as a guide to setting your room out but not every combination of TV watching and people will work within a rigid formula. You can always shuffle the furniture position a little to make sure it's working for everyone.

MAP IT OUT

Here's a guide to standard furniture sizes. Keep in mind, though, that this will vary depending on your style of furniture, but it's a good starting point.

- Couch
- 2.5-seater: 1900 mm
- 3-seater: 2100 mm
- 4-seater: 2600 mm
- Corner couch
- 2-seater with corner: 2200 mm x 2200 mm
- 3-seater with chaise: 3100 mm x 2100 mm
- Occasional chair: 900 mm x 900 mm
- Side table: 500 mm x 500 mm,
  600 mm x 600 mm
- Coffee table: 900 mm x 900 mm,
  1200 mm x 700 mm
- Rugs: 1700 mm x 2400 mm AND
  2000 mm x 3000 mm

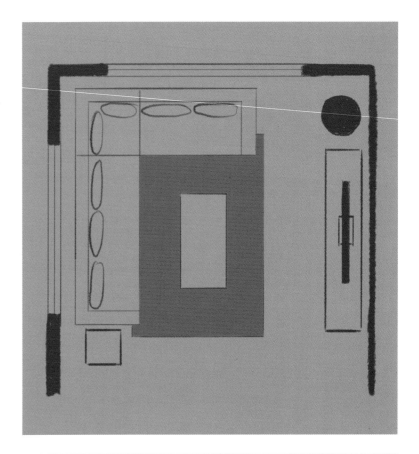

Move all your furniture out of the room (or all to one side), get a big roll of masking tape and map out the room. Stand in those positions, imagine sitting there and consider what you can see. Imagine surfing the channels, having a drink and where you would put the drink down, how close you will be to the next person and whether there is enough room for everyone. Make allowances for coffee tables and side tables to ensure the room will function at its best.

Do you have enough room for everything you envisage in your living room? You might be surprised.

COUCHES AND OCCASIONAL CHAIRS

A corner modular lounge suite is a good use of space within a room but gives a room more of a casual feel. Two couches in a corner layout with a small table in the corner or opposite each other can still feel relaxed, depending on the couch style. In general, a couch with a matching pair of occasional chairs seems formal; whereas a single occasional chair can add not only a relaxed feel but become a feature piece in the room.

POSITIONING

A common myth is that it's a faux pas to have the back of a couch facing those walking into the room. This comes from trying to create an 'open' feeling. As most of our rooms are now already open plan, we just have to accept that the couch is going to back onto some walkway or other. If the back of your couch is like a big visual 'block', you'll need to create something that will soften the view of a solid object.

A simple way to do this is to put a slim sofa table in front of the couch, with a few decorator items of staggering heights on top to break up the view. In a small area, this can also double up as a table to rest drinks on, which might mean you can do away with a side table.

Don't back your couches right up against the wall. This not only damages the walls but makes the room feel as though there isn't enough space for everything in it. By moving the couch even just 100 mm away from the wall, this will increase the sense of space in a room.

Where you have two large walls of windows, it is important that the couches don't sit right up against them, and by putting a distance of 400 mm between the couch and the window, you'll have easy access to the blinds. It will also make the lounge area feel more inviting and cosy – far better than having a huge expanse of floor in front of the couches.

We all love to cram as much furniture as possible into a room, filling every available nook and cranny, but I prefer to let a lounge room 'breathe'. Creating pockets of space, rather than filling them, actually makes a room feel bigger. It's like with congestion on a road: when cars are well spaced out, there is an even flow and you travel smoothly. Pack the cars all together in peak-hour traffic and you not only get congestion but frustration. This is the same in your lounge room: filling every corner is like creating congestion in your space and works against a relaxing feel.

When planning your furniture layout, consider side tables as much as coffee tables to give you flexibility.

CASE STUDY

I had a client whose lounge room was intended to be formal and not for everyday use, but which they still wanted to feel inviting. The owner had in mind a room they could bring people into for dinner, conversation or just to have a little quiet time.

There are some very strong lines in here with the fireplace, the rectangle in the rug, the defined hard lines in the arms of the chairs and the strong linear base of the lamps.

But look closely and you will see how prevalent the circle motif is. The artwork has a round shape, softening the harshness of the square picture frame and the fireplace. The coffee table is circular, bringing a sense of 'round table' mentality between the couch and the chairs. The sinewy, circular shapes in the pattern of the rug give a flow to the floor, taking the focus away from the shape of the rug and breaking up the strong lines of the timber flooring. Then you also have the same sort of sinewy pattern on the cushions.

Even though the placement of the chairs means they bookend the fireplace, the bit of movement in the pattern of the cushions gives a playful sense to the look. By having a circular drum-shaped shade, rather than square, on the lamps again the circular shape balances the strong lines of the bases.

Coffee tables and side tables are underrated pieces of furniture, and yet without them life is seriously disrupted: imagine sitting in a room without anywhere to rest your glass or place a bowl of chips. These tables make our rooms functional and help our living spaces operate seamlessly.

The distance between a coffee table and the couch should be a minimum of 500 mm. It can sit further away if there is a side table somewhere, but if it's the only surface in the room, having it out of easy reach from the couch makes things very uncomfortable.

A table doesn't have to come in the traditional form of four legs and a top. Ceramic stools function as a side table and a seat. An ottoman with trays can function as a footstool and table. A decorative chest can become an attractive and functional piece.

FLEXIBLE FUNCTION

The legs of this side table slide under the couch, making it the perfect 'TV dinner' table, and when not needed it moves to the side and sits over the arm of the couch.

Due to the unusual shape of this couch, the end tables were custom made to become an extension of the couch. The owners didn't want a permanent coffee table so two small tables were made with wheels: these can be pulled together and used when the room is in full entertaining mode.

The Showroom: RUGS

A rug is usually selected for its ability to add warmth, or to inject a bit of colour into an otherwise dull room. But a rug is more than an accessory: it can really define a space.

LARGE RUG

A large rug in an open living area creates a sense of intimacy. It acts like a signal that this area is for relaxing.

To make an area look bigger, put the rug under the couch legs so they connect with each other. Having the rug and couch in the same colours gives the illusion that the space is larger than it is, as you are joining the footprint of the rug and couch together.

BOLD RUG

This is a rug that says 'look at me', and with its bold palette it's hard to take your eyes off it. What this rug does is bring all the areas around it together. The colours link the artwork in the hallway, the red furniture and the green on the billiard table. This one rug connects three very important spaces in this house.

This client wanted to take a formal room at the front of the house and transform it into an instantly inviting, welcoming space. Nothing like a splash of colour and a billiard table to tell you this is a place that is not only full of fun and happiness, but will make you feel right at home straightaway.

LIGHTING

There are three types of lighting used within a home.

FUNCTIONAL LIGHTING: fixed overhead lighting that gives a general spill over the floor plan. This can come from downlights or pendant lighting. Pendant lighting needs to have a material that lets light through the fixture to give proper general or functional light.

TASK LIGHTING: this is directional lighting that performs a specific function, such as to aid reading, or improve visibility at a bench, a desk or the dining table.

ACCENT LIGHTING: this is also known as 'mood lighting', and is the most underrated form of lighting in a home. This can be in the form of candles, lamps, indirect lighting or through highlighting an object.

An average open plan room should have no more than 6–8 functional lights. I've seen a huge number of modern homes fitted with so many downlights that it's like being in a shopping centre! If you feel you need to see in every corner of the room – as though it is under interrogation – by all means add more, but ask your electrician to have them on separate switches so you can turn them on only if you have to.

All downlights will have different wattages, depending on the globe and output of the fixture. The number of lights you need will depend on the width of the beams, which is called the 'spill'. Without boring you by going into too much detail, I suggest you select a downlight with a wide beam for general use. This will minimise the total number of downlights you'll need.

If you tried to fill this corner with a chair or extra furniture, you would miss the area that allows the features in the room to breathe.

Long sheer curtains add elegance to a large room, and having them drape on the ground gives softness to any hard lines from timber flooring or angular cabinetry.

ENTERTAINMENT/PLAY ROOMS

What we do in our living spaces is varied. Sometimes it's a relaxed open area, the main venue for spending time with your family. But many of us are also keen to create media rooms, or play rooms (remember, it's not just kids who love a play room). There are extensions of the living room that have been grandly titled 'the entertainment room', which can include a billiard table, a bar and, of course, a TV.

To play is to take part in and occupy oneself with some amusement; it's about promoting fun, happiness and laughter. And, just as games have rules that are often tweaked or broken, the same goes for setting up entertainment areas in the home.

The basic rules of setting up an entertainment area are the same as for other living areas, but you have more licence to loosen up, and not have everything be purely functional. Yes, even though I firmly believe everything needs a proper function, I'm happy to bend the rules here.

I want you to use the rules and suggestions for the living space as a guide for your 'entertaining and play' areas, but go outside the box. As long as this space has the tools of play and the storage and seating sorted, it should be completely open when it comes to how it's executed. Put the initial emphasis on storage and ensure there are enough seats and tables, and then turn a blind eye to the fun mess that happens when you play without rules. All you have to do is shut the door and enjoy.

Time to play!

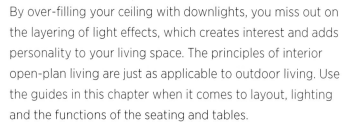

By over-filling your ceiling with downlights, you miss out on the layering of light effects, which creates interest and adds personality to your living space. The principles of interior open-plan living are just as applicable to outdoor living. Use the guides in this chapter when it comes to layout, lighting and the functions of the seating and tables.

COMBINING LIGHTING

A mixture of downlights in the ceiling and a pendant in the corner creates many moods and layers to this entertaining room.

FLOOR LAMPS

A decorative floor lamp is a functional task light that can be moved to accommodate reading or looking carefully at something on the table, but it can also be used as a mood light when you're sitting in other parts of the room.

MOOD

Creating shadows by putting a light behind a solid object can transform a simple piece into a feature.

ACCENT LIGHTING

A dramatic overhead light on a sculptural vase not only creates a mood within a room but means you can leave the main lights off at night while watching TV.

LAMPS

These glowing 'pebble' lights let off a soft glow and set a mood within the room.

CANDLES

Never underestimate the elegance candlelight can give to a room.

RULES ROUND-UP

- Map out your room. Do a plan drawing to scale or map it out physically with masking tape.

- Look at the standard sizes of furniture that fit within the shape of the room to make sure you don't overstuff it.

- Measure the distance around a coffee table to make sure you can easily move around it.

- Make sure you have the optimum distance between furniture and your TV.

- Include two to three different types of lighting in the room and don't use too many ceiling lights.

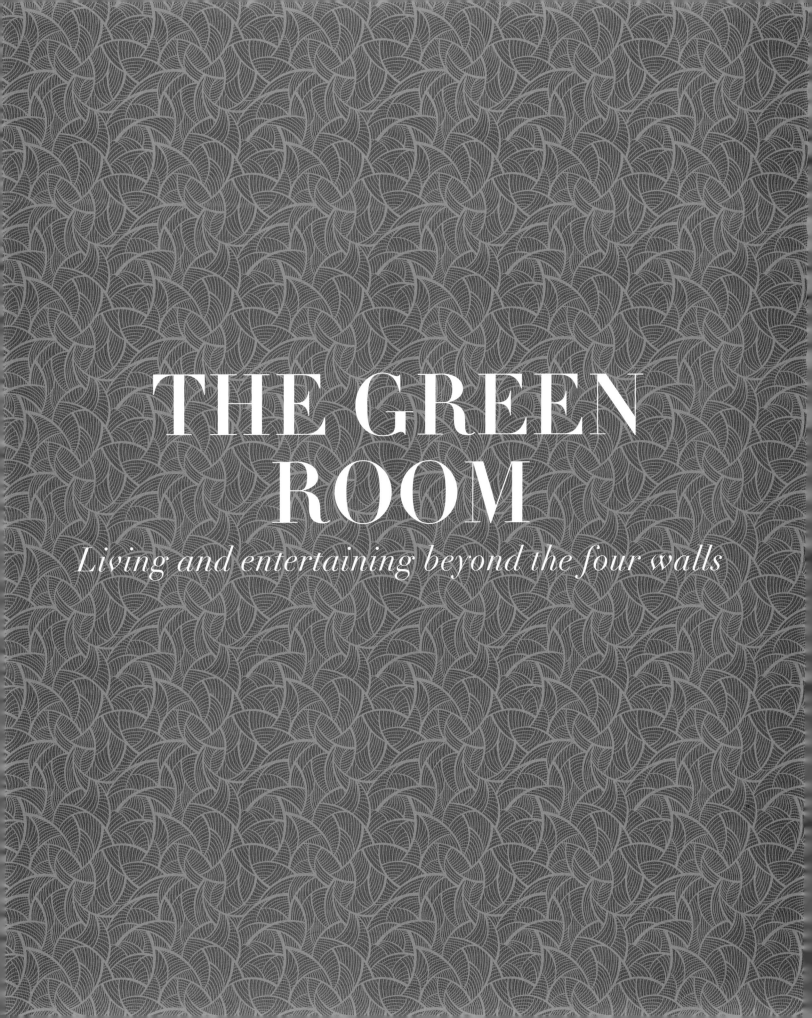

THE GREEN ROOM

Living and entertaining beyond the four walls

THE GREEN ROOM

These days, the line between inside and outside is blurred. The old trend of using a lonely houseplant to bring a little of the outdoors in has been completely turned around. Often our houses now feature an expanse of windows not only to make the most of natural light but to frame nature's artwork.

Thinking about the vista from your lounge room or kitchen has become a complex activity: what is outside needs to complement and balance what you have inside. Sound tough? With a little help, it won't seem as foreboding. Whether your exterior is an extension of the home's interior scheme or it's used as a dramatic focal point, the two areas have to be thought of as one. You can't ignore the impact our outdoor spaces have on both our everyday living and the look of our interiors.

The biggest change in recent house designs has been the emphasis on outdoor living spaces, which can be anything from the humble pergola with an outdoor table and barbecue, up to an area decked out with big-screen TVs and full surround-sound.

Because we so often entertain outdoors these days, the focus has shifted away from the once 'must-have' theatre room and bumped the rumpus room even further down the wish list. We no longer look for huge homes extending right to the back fence, taking up all the land; we are aiming to create liveable spaces in our gardens that enhance indoor living.

That said, any dreams of half-acre plots of land are long gone. We have learnt instead to use our surrounding parks and urban gardens, as the boundaries of the inner city stretch further out into the suburbs. Typically, blocks of land are smaller and we are living closer to each other: we're using our land more practically, somewhere for living and entertaining rather than the place to host a cricket match or a kick of the footy. Align that with our increased awareness about water conservation and sustainability issues, as well as our desire to grow our own produce, and it's clear we are packing more into the one space than ever before.

A ROOM WITH A VIEW

Design in the home revolves around focal points and places to which the eye is naturally drawn. For instance, the view outside any large window will command attention, but the interior still has to have its own individual features. You will always need something that attracts the gaze when the blinds are closed or once it's night-time and you can't see what is going on outdoors. In saying that, a mesmerising view is always going to be the 'hero' in the battle between focal points, so it is important that the interior plays the perfect supporting role to bring out the best in what is beyond the wall of glass.

A great way to build a connection between inside and out is with colour. Nature is the perfect inspiration: look to the trunks of trees or the lush leaves and flowers of shrubs and plants. Green is always dominant in the landscape but when decorating an entertaining area, use the items closer to the window as the basis of your colour scheme. The structure of the pergola, decorative pots or furniture can be used as your link.

BEFORE AND AFTER – CASE STUDY

BEFORE: On walking into this lounge area, you noticed three points: the lounge, the decking and the massive studio above the garage. The owners were frustrated that they had this beautiful entertaining space which felt dominated by the wall of steel above the garage. The goal was to make the lounge and the garden the focus so visitors were drawn into the area to eat, drink, laugh – and not left wanting to get the hell out of there within minutes.

AFTER: Establishing the point of focus was the first step in building layers in this area. The bright fabrics on the new seating area instantly draw you in and direct the eye away from the dominant shape of the studio. A criss-cross of stainless-steel wires were put in over the full height of the balustrade, so in a couple of years it will be a wall of tumbling evergreen vines and fragrant flowers in spring and summer. The introduction of greenery softened the industrial steel and turned this space into a tranquil garden rather than an architectural structure.

Because the decking and seating area is so prominent, it is important that the colours inside have a direct relationship to the exterior to help to achieve a seamless, polished look.

Here are some examples of how this can work. By playing with the colour connections, you can create echoes across outdoor and indoor spaces. I worked on an outdoor space where a dominant water feature and large amounts of timber were the most eye-catching components. In painting the interior room a dark colour, this helped to frame what was going on outside: the charcoal beams on the pergola structure linked back to the walls' blue-black. The outdoor cushions I selected were a monochromatic pattern, creating another subtle link to the interior. The two spaces were connected through the colour choices, but the outside was a more relaxed version of the formal interior.

In another client's house, I encountered a rendered side wall of an outdoor area that looked quite harsh and heavy when combined with a solid timber deck. Planting natural bamboo in front of the wall softened the look, with its delicate leaves forming a gentle moving screen. We stopped the flooring short of the wall to make

room for a sunken garden bed. The columns on the side were rendered in a rough texture and applied with a rusted paint finish, framing the mini garden. From the lounge room, this became a living 3-D wall sculpture. Lights in the bases of the pots created a wall of shadows and colour, making it a feature in the evening as well.

Inner-city living puts up many obstacles between you and the perfect view from your windows: trying to block out that two-storey house next door is an epic challenge. But you don't have to build a wall a mile high to hide what's behind it. Rather than worrying about completely obscuring the building you can see out your window, think of ways to create interest at eye level. A set of screens won't block out the entirety of the house next door, but they will attract your focus so that you'll notice whatever sits immediately in front of the window. Using a screen will draw your eye to any plants or pots you keep in front of it, and mean that you will hardly notice what's looming behind.

THE EXTENDED
ENTERTAINING AREA

While you want to emphasise the relationship between the outdoor room and the interior, you need to keep them distinct; otherwise you may as well put up windows and doors everywhere. The beauty of the outdoor space is that you are protected to a certain degree but still get the benefits of fresh air and being outside. All materials, furniture and surfaces should be chosen carefully as they will get wet, dusty and have to withstand harsh sun and the cold. Surfaces will fade, be vulnerable to mould and get the odd 'present' from birds wandering into your space.

It used to be that a pergola was an area made up of a couple of beams with a place to grow some vines that maybe gave up a few grapes. Now it's the case that these structures are more often drawn up in conjunction with a whole team of interior designers, architects and landscapers. When you are dealing with these types of structures it becomes more of a building or extension project, of a larger scale than putting on decking, so keep in mind that all normal building regulations will apply.

Putting on a roof doesn't instantly make an area waterproof, so if you are looking at having your Green Room more like a full-on entertainment space with TVs, surround sound and free of the elements, engaging a designer or draftsperson should be your first port of call. Find out what your local council restrictions/requirements are with regard to square footage, roof heights and how close you can go to neighbouring fences.

Creating a structure like this isn't cheap so do your sums before construction: it can cost anywhere between $10K and $100K, depending on how extravagant you want to be. But, remember, your excitement could lead to you overcapitalising so be aware of the size of houses and median prices in your area so you can remain realistic about how much you should sink into your Green Room.

This house had a modern interior, while the house next door was made of old-fashioned hand-tumbled red bricks. The bricks inspired the aged style of the pots. If the pots were a solid colour and highly glazed, they would have looked too modern and out of place.

FURNITURE AND LAYOUT

So what types of parties do you like having? When we move out the back door and sit outside, it is always a party of some sort. Whether you are taking time out with a pot of tea and a magazine or gathering a hundred guests to celebrate a twenty-first, an outdoor space is all about entertaining. Take into consideration the types of entertaining you want to do in your outdoor area and gear the look of your space towards them.

As with our lounging and dining areas, you need to take into consideration the width and depth of your fixed flooring area. It's pretty hard to change the square footage when you have fences and sides of houses to contend with. The spatial requirements are exactly the same as inside the home, so use the layout information from the dining and living chapters as a guide to the sizes of tables, types of chairs the clearance space you need around them, and if you can or can't fit built-in seating.

Outdoor living is all about flexibility so make sure your furniture fits your space comfortably. Choose modular couches that can change their shape and layout, and tables that can be moved to different areas depending on how they can be best used.

A huge decking area built for everyday barbecues and lounging was transformed into a sit-down venue for sixty people.

The Showroom: ROOFS

There are many ways to make an outdoor space look layered: with roofing, screening and sides that open and close. A Green Room should be flexible in how it controls the light, heat and natural airflow. The whole reason behind a roofed area is to protect it from the elements so you can leave your furniture outside and none of your guests will have to bolt inside whenever it looks like there'll be a spot of rain. There are a vast number of options available: a full plastered roof, an open-beam structure with laser lights, using shutters that direct the sun and airflow, or a combination of these options.

PLASTERED ROOF

A full plastered roof with fixed lighting adds square footage to your living and entertaining space. The benefits of a solid roof include full protection from harsh UV rays and any conditions the weather can throw at you. The downside is that the eave will block out more and more natural light the deeper it extends.

In this renovation, the bonus of having windows above the roofline meant we could go out as far out as we wanted, without sacrificing all the natural light.

POLYCARBONATE ROOF

The beauty of this roof is its light, waterproof structure, and the fact it doesn't block any light streaming into the house. The downside is that it generates a lot of heat during summer. There needs to be good airflow through the space to move out the hot stale air and some type of shade structure is recommended if you want to make full use of it.

You can use shadecloth that is fixed to the beams for around 30 per cent protection, or else you can opt for solid retractable blinds. These blinds are made from a block-out material but they do trap the heat, so you will stop the direct light going into the area but it will still be hot.

LOUVRE BLINDS

Exterior ceiling louvre blinds protect you from the elements like a solid roof would, but have the flexibility of being opened like normal window shutters to let in light and fresh air.

BENCH SEAT

A high-backed bench seat doubles up in terms of its function. It creates a half wall and becomes a fully protected wall when the café blinds are pulled down. The clear material allows full light to flood into the area.

SHUTTERS

Solid shutters protect from all the elements, including the sun, and help direct airflow on those hot days.

SUN SCREEN

The sun doesn't always come in overhead. Vertical sun-screen blinds protect surfaces and reduce heat when the sun moves.

CASSETTE SCREEN

'Cassette' fitted screens are easy to open and close, without any fussy cords to contend with and give an airtight fit as they are secured to the beams.

FENCE

This 2.7 m high fence gives privacy from the neighbours. The vertical slats in alternate widths give a decorative finish to the screen, and double as a backdrop for the growing plants.

VERTICAL DIVIDERS

You could call them walls, but I consider these to be more like dividers: this speaks to how flexible and useful they can be. Not only can dividers offer protection from the elements but they can cleverly demarcate areas, such as your neighbour's house, or screen off a bad view. All the while preserving a full open-air experience. The options when it comes to dividers are varied – and much nicer than the ones you might find at your office!

SURFACES AND MATERIALS

We're talking about outdoor areas and all the spontaneous drinks nights, long Sunday lunches and casual get-togethers that we like to host there. If you find yourself getting stressed out about what might happen if your guests don't use coasters or placemats at a barbecue, you might

be missing the point. It's good to keep the big picture in mind here – no matter how big or glamorous, this should be a relaxed and casual entertaining space.

That doesn't mean you want people to be disrespectful of your property, but we all have to accept that tables will get marked and fabrics will get stained, no matter how weather-resistant the material on the seats and cushions. Blown-in leaves and bark will settle on the furniture, and if they get wet, a natural resin can leach out and leave marks that can't always be removed. Timbers will age and weather, leaves will blow in and dust will settle on every surface possible – these are eternal truths and it's better not to fight them.

An outdoor area shouldn't be thought of as somewhere that must be kept in pristine condition at all costs but a place that will look even better with weathering and use.

Not only is stainless steel perfect for a chef's kitchen, it is my number-one choice for an exterior barbecue. With a built-in sink as well, you can be as messy as you want and wipe it down without worrying about the mess, the smell or the stains.

Stone is one our most durable surfaces, and as stone wears it gives history to a piece of furniture. Stone is porous and it will be affected by spills, especially liquids with an acid base, so if you are doing tequila shots or hosting red-wine tasting nights maybe bring out some fancy chopping boards to set the glasses on to reduce the chance of marking.

Laminated benches are perfect for indoors and can work just as well outdoors, but they need protection from the elements to prevent the boards swelling. A tip is to watch the direction of any nearby shutters so that when it's wet, the rain doesn't fall onto the interior bench material.

DECKS

There are many types of flooring that will give you a good sturdy base for outdoor entertaining, from the cheapest stained pine or lacquered planks to exotic hardwoods. Your budget will determine how much decking you have and the type of timber you will use.

Pine is a soft timber that sustains dints and imperfections very easily, whereas Australian hardwoods such as spotted gum, blackbutt and jarrah not only have a dense, hard-wearing structure, but are also termite-resistant. If humidity is a problem where you live, you'll need to keep in mind not only the hardness of the timber but its ability to resist mould: the coatings you use and level of maintenance you're willing to do are just as important as the timber type.

Is your family big on barbecues? If so, oil and fats will be your biggest enemy. Maintenance is the key to keeping stains minimal on your deck.

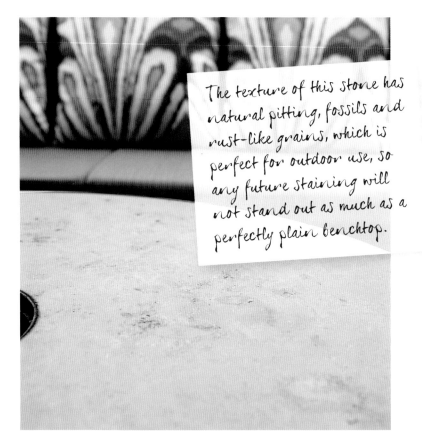

The texture of this stone has natural pitting, fossils and rust-like grains, which is perfect for outdoor use, so any future staining will not stand out as much as a perfectly plain benchtop.

The beauty of timber is, of course, its sanding and resurfacing qualities, which means it usually doesn't take more than some good old-fashioned elbow grease to get it looking great again.

There are a couple of brands of timber prep cleaner that can rejuvenate tired and weathered decking, and these are also perfect for removing stains caused by fats and foods. There is no guarantee of getting the stains out so once again keep at the front of your mind that this is an outdoor space. Imperfections not only give a lived-in look but build a space's character. If you have timber chairs and tables, the same prep products can be used to bring them back to life.

We have a big timber table at home with quite a few telltale cup rings that just won't disappear; I look at these as reminders of good times shared with friends over a few drinks.

CONCRETE AND PAVING

If you don't want to worry about maintenance or looking after timber, a slab of concrete is the way to go. Seal the concrete or cover it with paving paint and when it starts to look a little worn, give it another coat; simple with no fuss! Take it to the next level and get the concrete stamped with patterns to look like paving. Another alternative is a surface spray that creates a textured finish which has lines added to it to look like paving. These of course are all surfaces that you would employ a contractor/business to do rather than a DIY project.

Putting in real pavers is a more detailed job and requires focus and effort at the preparation stage. First, you need to lay a sub-base of stone and sand for drainage; this is then compacted to give a sturdy base. The preparation of the base is absolutely essential as pavers move and can become unstable over time. If the base isn't laid correctly, you might find yourself having to re-do the whole area in a couple of years' time. Depending on the pavers this can be an expensive process so if you don't know what you are doing, I would highly recommend getting a professional to lay your pavers. This will not only ensure you get the perfect result, it'll save a lot of hassle in the long run.

The beauty of outdoor areas is all you need to do is squirt them with a hose and give them a going-over with a soft broom to freshen them up. Keep the wire-brush scrubbing and water-pressure-washers for pavers and concrete only, as they are too harsh for the natural fibres of decking timbers.

SEATING

Built-in seating and benchtops are becoming standard features in structured outdoor areas. As these are fixtures, the construction needs to be tackled in the same way as you would when commissioning a piece of customised interior furniture or specialised kitchen cabinetry. Having seating and benches tailor-made gives a unique and individual element to your Green Room.

As with a typical indoor seat, the depths and heights of a bench seat need to be built to proper seating standards. A seat between 450–500 mm high is standard, but because the bench seat is more about casual lounging, the depth usually varies between 400 and 600 mm. This, of course, can be deeper if you're after more of a daybed feel. A depth of 600 mm for a bench seat accommodates extra-plump cushions to lean on.

A foam cushion can be anywhere between 50 and 100 mm in thickness, so make allowances for this when building a fixed bench seat. To get the best results you can make the bench seats a project for yourself or get your builder/cabinetmaker to build them for you. As for the padding, you can get foam cut from a foam/rubber supplier and sew the covers yourself or get a professional upholsterer to do it for you.

The technology of fabrics and inserts has come a long way, meaning our outdoor spaces can be water-, weather- and sun-proof, and all without a piece of vinyl in sight! Marine upholstery wadding and foam has worked for decades in boats but having these covered in vinyl really gives an outdoor area a dated 1970s or caravan feel. That's fine if your theme is retro-caravan but today's outdoor areas are more about replicating the interior, and that includes easy living comfort, anywhere from casual to a luxury environment.

Guarantees on outdoor fabrics vary from five to seven years, depending on whether they are left outside permanently. No matter what the guarantees state, unless your space is fully protected from direct sunlight and rain, I'd suggest you put the soft furnishings in storage over the cooler months and only bring them out when the sun starts shining and you're actually using them. This will extend the lives of your products. If the soft furnishings were the only splashes of colour in the outdoor area, look to winter-flowering plants to inject some life and vibrancy back into the space.

> If the soft furnishings are the only splashes of colour in the outdoor area, look to winter-flowering plants to inject some life and vibrancy back into the space.

The great thing about fixed seats is not only the extra storage they provide but the hidden features you can build into them. My favourite example of this is a seat containing a hardwired esky, complete with a full supply of drinks for a barbecue, and all without having to compromise cupboard storage. After all, having guests staring into the fridge isn't really what you want in an outdoor area.

These cushions are a stunning feature of the outdoor area and are left out for most of the summer months. But when winter comes the lift-up storage keeps everything water-tight and protected.

The Showroom: HEATING

FIRE PIT

Today's fire pits go beyond the old rusted gallon drum and are in fact sophisticated sculptural works when not in use. This backyard was all about designating the space as somewhere for conversation, with the fire bowl as the central focus. When the fire isn't in use, a removable case is put over the top, and it doubles as a coffee table. The pebbled ring area not only looks great but reduces the maintenance of the lawn. The chairs are made of recycled plastic and are marine-strength powder-coated so they can stay in position full time. A splash of temporary colour in the cushions turns this easygoing functional area into a fashion statement.

GAS HEATER

Only a fully weatherproof area can take on a gas heater. These heaters run on mains gas or, as this one does, on LP gas. Running a new gas line could add significant cost if your heater is away from a main gas line. Using gas bottles can be more economical than full connection costs.

ETHANOL HEATER

Ethanol heaters can pump out a lot of heat and this mini-cylinder heater gives a punch of warmth into long nights spent sitting outside. To boot, the coffee table is a functional work of art that acts as a talking point.

PORTABLE HEATER

Popular in cafés, the portable heater is great for bringing indoor comfort outside, but be aware that if you have one in a closed-in area, as with any gas appliance, you must comply with manufacturers' ventilation requirements and ceiling-height restrictions.

STRIP HEATING

I have terrible memories of the electric-strip heaters in our bathroom – the sort that would burn you if you got too close – but these modern versions are sophisticated and sleek. Again, taking their lead from outdoor cafés, these are a lot more streamlined than the old clunky portable heaters. When buying, be aware of the electrical requirements and whether these heaters will need their own circuit. What could look to be an elegant addition to your outdoor area could end up costing you thousands when you have to upgrade your electrical mains meter.

HEATING

Depending on the type of structure you have, your heating options are almost endless, although I do draw the line at ducted heating! There is something mesmerising about an open fire, and with the majority of interior fireplaces being replaced by gas, a fire pit and an outdoor flame take us back to the days of campfires and Billy Tea.

GARDEN POCKETS

The best thing about a garden is it helps you to feel connected to the outside world. You don't need to have a huge backyard to do this, but creating little pockets of magic outside can really change the feel of the space.

A well-designed piece of furniture, such as a bench seat in the front yard, becomes a sculptural feature to visually add to a space as well as being a place to chill and relax.

Create nooks in your yard which capture the morning sun. A perfect place for the morning paper and tea.

Your Green Room is an extension of the interior whether you are using it as extra seating, somewhere to entertain, or just as a view to get lost in as you stare out your window. Even if you just have one pot with a few herbs, it'll give you a connection with the outdoors. It is a completely different sensory experience to your interior space and should be treated that way.

RULES ROUND-UP

- Figure out whether you are creating a small area or a structure that needs building approval.

- Decking isn't the only flooring option available.

- Which elements, such as wind, rain and sun, do you need protection from? Which flexible options can provide it?

- Is the view the focus from inside the house, and if so what do you need to do to connect the interior and exterior?

- Make sure you know how much the whole project will cost so you don't overcapitalise.

- Customised seating is a start to making your Green Room unique.

- If you spend a lot of time entertaining, look at hidden storage.

- Seating, tables and flooring outside takes a lot rougher treatment than indoors, so research your surfaces.

- Plan your space to be flexible for intimate settings as well as entertaining on a large scale.

LAUNDRY

The forgotten room – our dirty little secret

LAUNDRY

Over the decades, the laundry has gone up and down in our collective estimation. It is a part of the house not valued for its beauty but its function – if our kitchen is the warm heart of the home, the laundry is the often-forgotten metabolism that keeps us ticking along. It keeps our hidden tools like brooms, mops, buckets, vacuum cleaners and laundry baskets. It's where you'll find all the bleaches, powders, cleaning products and liquids the nature of which you're not quite sure about but figure should stay at the back of the cupboard anyway. You'll also find in there a spare of anything,

lightbulbs, that bulky 48-pack of toilet rolls and the 'lost sock home'. It is also a great place to put the dog food and kitty litter (a much nicer spot than the guest bathroom; just a little hint there). Depending on its size, the laundry can even be a mini repair centre, a place to store the sewing machine with its collection of bits and bobs.

On the other end of the spectrum is the dream laundry: a space that boasts built-in ironing-boards, spacious drying cupboards and a muck room for wet boots, jackets and school bags. But with the square-footage demands that come with

having larger kitchens, living spaces and bath-rooms, choosing a smaller laundry seems like an easy way to save space.

Put the extra effort into planning your laundry so your dining table is left for eating at, instead of sorting out the ironing.

To do the basics, a laundry doesn't even have to be separate room any more. With more of us living in the inner city (and the smaller spaces this entails), and the European influence on house design, you will often find that 'laundry' really means 'a washing machine behind a door in a kitchen or bathroom'. If you think this is a little measly, you might end up just being grateful it's still in the house and not in a separate outbuilding in the backyard.

No matter the size or where you find it, a functional laundry needs to accommodate the following:

- Soaking
- Washing big/tall items
- Washing machine
- Dryer
- Area to dry/hang washing
- Drying room
- Ironing
- Storage
- Folding/sorting

Of course, not all these actions/appliances are confined to the one space, but nevertheless they need to be done *somewhere*, and this should to be taken into consideration when designing or reno-vating a house. By listing all these actions, you can make sure a space is allocated to each one. It might be that you store everything in the laundry and do the ironing somewhere else. But if you like to hide away while doing the ironing, you'll have to consider the amount of space needed for this.

SOAKING

Most of us will need to regularly soak clothing, either to remove stains or handwash delicate items, so a tub in a laundry is essential. If you are soak-ing something overnight, you could use a sizable bucket so you aren't taking up the laundry tub for a long period of time. It can be tricky if your laundry doesn't have a tub, but soaking clothing can easily be done in the bathroom or kitchen. In those cases, you'll definitely need to create a system for handwashing so you don't keep the tub full of water and stop it being used for other things. The basin or even your bath can be used for handwashing and hanging out the odd item, but if this is a shared area, as in a flat or the fam-ily's main bathroom, be aware that not everyone will appreciate you leaving your smalls hanging up there for too long.

BIG/TALL ITEMS

There are lots of odd-shaped things about the house that need the occasional clean but which won't fit in the kitchen sink: think of tall vases, bike wheels and even the family dog. And, if you have a bike rider in the house who's precious about their machine, the humble outside tap just won't suffice.

It's essential to take these factors into consideration when selecting the size of your tub; if it's the same size as your kitchen sink, you really aren't gaining any advantage. You'll also need to consider the height and type of your laundry tap, ensuring that the biggest item you can imagine washing will fit under it. If you don't accommodate that, I guarantee you will be using the outside tap to wash some pretty important items (and we already know a certain cyclist won't be happy!). I find that wall-mounted laundry taps are perfect, but make sure they swivel and have a good hob shape to them so that things can slip under the outlet easily.

WASHING MACHINE

The first decision to make here is whether you'll have a top-loading or front-loading washing machine. Some front loaders can also act as a steam press or double as dryers as well, so they can be a great dual-functional choice.

Make sure you look at the items you wash often and get the machine that will best accommodate them. Also, think about the size of your family and how many times a week the washing machine will be used. Going for a large machine with a five-year warranty will get you through the tough times with little kids, muddy sports players and endless loads of towels and sheets. These sorts of machines do take up a bit of extra space, though, so if it's just the two of you, remember that bigger isn't always better. Don't waste precious space or spend money when you don't need to.

I have a pet hate when it comes to front loaders: bending down and dragging out the heavy wet items. This problem can be avoided by raising front loaders off ground level, supported by a braced shelf. This means you can have the basket sitting on the ground underneath the machine and just drop all the items into it, rather than dragging them around, straining your back in the process.

If you're tall enough, it can be a good idea to have the dryer sitting above the washing machine. That way, you'll have both machines in a line and be able to store the basket underneath.

Of course, these machines are hefty and when filled with water and clothes they are incredibly heavy. You have to make sure your builder and cabinetmaker work together to create a support structure on the wall and the appropriate bracing for the shelf. It's worth the effort: a raised washing machine leaves plenty of free bench space and creates the perfect spot to store the empty washing basket.

DRYER

I gave up my dryer ten years ago and can honestly say I've never missed it. It means you think ahead, you don't leave your washing to the last minute and, of course, it saves you a ton on electricity.

The amount of steam a dryer generates in a laundry also affects the longevity of your cabinetry and can cause mildew on the walls and ceilings. If you do have a dryer, make sure you have proper ventilation by way of either a fan or a window that opens so condensation doesn't build up.

Washing machines and dryers can look like they have disappeared completely if they are hidden away behind cabinetry doors in a laundry, kitchen or bathroom. But remember to leave the cabinet doors open for proper ventilation when they are operating.

HANGING AND DRYING

As I don't have a dryer and sunshine just can't be relied on where we live, sometimes we have to hang our clothes somewhere other than the clothesline. An outdoor area with a roof is our friend when it comes to clothes drying, and in the depths of winter we use the clothes horse in the spare room. Not the ideal decorative item but it's a compromise I've willingly made in choosing not to have a dryer. An alternative is to install a small ceiling-mounted clothes airer, which is operated using pulleys. These are perfect for apartment buildings, or when you don't have access to that spare room in which to hide your washing.

If you have space, a drying room is the ultimate laundry fixture. This is less a 'room' than a large cabinet, and there are two types. One is a finished cabinet that plugs into an electrical socket; your clothes dry as the airflow circulates within. This uses up about the same amount of energy as a conventional dryer, so if you're looking for an energy-saver, this isn't exactly the right item for you.

The other type is a cabinet purpose built by your cabinet-maker that has a duct directed from your heating into the cavity. When you have the heating on, it dries your clothes at the same time. I have heard people say, 'But that means I can't use it in summer.' My theory is if you don't need a heater on, then you'd be putting your washing on the line anyway.

The great thing about a drying room is that it will easily accommodate large jackets and boots – perfect for skiers and hikers. I can't see why you couldn't dry sleeping bags and large doonas in there as well. Those items take a long time to dry and aren't suitable for dryers, so I think a drying room would be a good inclusion for a busy family that does a lot of camping and outdoor activities.

No matter the size of your laundry, allowing space for folding, hanging and drying keeps the rest of the house laundry-free.

HOMEMADE DRYING CABINET

Now, this is just a little DIY tip from me to you! In one of my last houses, we had ducted heating in the flooring. My trick was to put the clothes horse over the duct, hang the clothes and then put over the top a fitted sheet which trapped all the heat. The mini hot-air balloon this created was quite entertaining for little kids *and* it got all my drying done in no time.

Beautiful to look at? Not at all, but if it's raining outside and you don't have a dryer, you have to get creative.

We now have ducted heating in the ceiling, which I don't find to be the best type and it's also ruined my invention. I have been guilty of attaching the odd hanger to the vent to quickly dry a shirt or two. But leaving the hanger in the vent full time for convenience's sake is a cardinal sin when it comes to decorating, so make sure when the items are dry to move them along quick-smart. Otherwise, you'll be in danger of getting used to it and not noticing the dangling eyesore till someone comes to visit and points it out. Save yourself the embarrassment and get it back in the cupboard, where it belongs!

IRONING

I feel like in this section I'm airing all my own dirty laundry, but here it is: I don't iron. When I was a first-time mum, I wanted everything to be perfect; I would iron little jumpsuits, singlets, blankets, sheets – everything really. You can imagine the stress I caused myself trying to keep up with that workload.

When I started back at work and the kids were still little, I allowed myself the luxury of having an ironing lady come in once a fortnight. The joy of seeing everything neatly pressed on hangers truly was my guilty pleasure. Trouble was, when our finances got a little tight, the ironing lady was the first to go. By that stage, I had become used to not putting aside time for the task. Instead of frantically trying to keep up with the ironing, though, I gave it up altogether! I unchained myself from the ironing basket and, I can tell you, it set me free. Yes, the kids occasionally go out wearing wrinkled T-shirts despite my smoothing down everything that comes off the line before folding, but for me saying goodbye to ironing was truly liberating.

Clearly, allowing a lot of room for ironing is just not up there on my priority list; we do have an iron and board, but they only come out when we really need them.

Let's all admit that ironing is boring.

Of course, I know there are many people who would never dream of giving up ironing. For them, there's quite a lot to consider: not just the iron and the board, but the ironing basket too. This basket will always have something in it and can't double as the laundry basket for clothes brought in from the line. You can't get away with it being the same place that the dirty clothes are stored either. If you are a dyed-in-the-wool ironer, more than likely you have an area for sorting your clothes as well.

This means you'll need space for three baskets, minimum. These can be on display openly as a three-basket area, or you can keep them under the laundry bench.

Either way, it means a lot of room being taken up in your laundry. Baskets can really cut into your storage space so be aware of the minimum size and number you need to make your ironing routines happen smoothly.

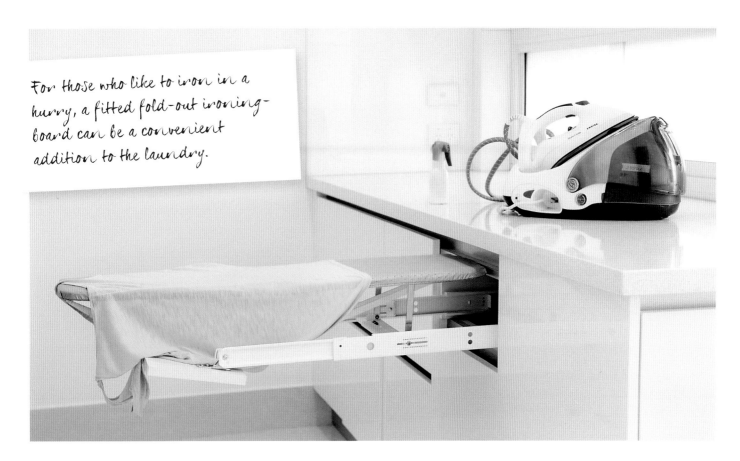

For those who like to iron in a hurry, a fitted fold-out ironing-board can be a convenient addition to the laundry.

This laundry is quite small and unassuming, but by putting in colourful, playful wallpaper and bold colours, the space feels fun, and less like a 'room of doom'.

Look at your options when it comes to basket size: it could be a case of using small or stackable baskets so you are only taking up one cupboard space. This should then leave you with one basket permanently sitting on the bench, or on an open shelf or on top of your cabinets, if they don't go right up to the ceiling. What you want to avoid is having the basket end up in the middle of the floor, constantly getting shuffled around, which is just plain annoying.

Let's all admit that ironing is boring, and having to fight with a 'testy' ironing-board that seems to want to adjust to its own height no matter how much you coax the legs into your preferred spot, is a big enough reason for me to give up before I have even started. The solution? A built in ironing-board is so convenient, and slides out with ease. The thought of no long risking being twisted between an ironing-board's legs might even be enough to entice me back into the 'fold'.

FOLDING AND SORTING

If you are one of those super-organised types who does the folding and sorting at the line, making piles in the basket all ready to go straight to the right room or person to be put away, then I commend you! If that doesn't happen, you'll need space to sort out the contents of the basket. You might have enough room in your laundry to include a bench for this purpose. If bench space is limited, you could get small pull-out shelves installed just under the bench, giving you extra resting space for the piles you've already folded.

More often than not the kitchen table or couch becomes the proxy sorting area, and sometimes this becomes a permanent fixture. I don't have any magic interior designer's solutions for this one, unfortunately. With some luck, though, the tips I've offered so far might help you to put some plans into action so you get the laundry off the kitchen table. Then the family can start using it as it was intended – for eating!

STORAGE

The laundry really needs to accommodate all the awkwardly shaped and sized objects that don't seem to belong anywhere else. You know the ones: they inevitably find their way to the laundry, turning it into a mini dumping ground. Write a list of what you already keep in the laundry, and then create a wish list cataloguing what you actually *want* to store in there. Is there anything on the first list that could be stored in the shed or garage? At my house, a lot of sports equipment tends to get dumped in the laundry. Unless it's something that gets used every day, I find the garage is the better place to store these sorts of items.

A tall cabinet is essential in a laundry, or is it?

Mops, brooms and ironing-boards often get shoved into tall cupboards, hidden from sight, which sounds perfect, but what if you are short on bench space? It's worth asking yourself which would you prefer: a tall cupboard or more bench space? A rare lucky few will have a laundry with cupboards on both sides of the room; in this case, the wall in between can be a great place for hanging storage. Using brackets into which you snap broom and mop handles and rest the ironing-board, will free up valuable cupboard space in a laundry.

The tiles were selected to match the colours of the wallpaper.

You have to spend time in the laundry, so give it impact with colour.

Stacking the washing machine, dryer and basket all in one makes room for more bench and storage space in a tiny laundry.

Deep cupboards are perfect for storing the body of your vacuum cleaner while you hang the hose in the upright cupboard or on a wall bracket.

I love having vases at hand but the trouble is they are bulky and hard to store. Open shelving is ideal for keeping the good ones on display but use above-bench cupboards for basic, nondescript vases.

The laundry is like a chemical playground and even if you don't have small children of your own, make sure you store the powders and chemicals up high. Keeping them tucked away in a cupboard is easy but you can also have fun with the containers and make them a feature of your decorating.

Spending time in the laundry can make you feel as though you've been delegated the most boring job in the world, so why not give the space a bit of colour and excitement?

The laundry may not be the most interesting room in your home, but if you tick all the essential boxes, it will run smoothly. This will give you time to focus on the other areas of the house that are more important to you.

RULES ROUND-UP

- Use all available wall space, with cabinetry extending to the ceiling.

- Look at how you can get the most bench space in your laundry.

- Can you save storage space by hanging your tall items, such as brooms and mops, on the wall?

- Ventilation by either fans or open windows is a must with dryers.

- Decide between a front loader or top loader and ask yourself whether a dryer is really necessary.

- Put some fun into the laundry using colour.

- Include slide-out baskets for sorting washing from items to be folded or ironed.

BATHROOM

Water therapy for the soul

BATHROOM

When we were growing up, our bathroom was no more than a utility room – a place in which you'd jockey with the rest of the family to try to see yourself in the mirror while brushing your teeth. In our house, there was one bathroom and one toilet, a tiny cabinet for the essentials, a basin and pedestal, complete with exposed plumbing, and a shower over the bath. You'd dash to the bathroom in the morning, screaming, 'I'm first!', and if you were lucky, you'd get a shower before the hot water ran out.

I know some people still have bathrooms like this. If you do, please don't imagine that I think you live in the dark ages, but when it comes time to renovate, or build or buy a new house, I can guarantee the minimum you'll want will be a main bathroom *and* an ensuite off the master bedroom. If there's no ensuite, there should at least be a second toilet. It doesn't have to be a huge space but having more than one toilet will guarantee a better price for your home, if or when you come to sell it. If you have a two-storey house, a powder room is considered a necessity. This will mean visitors won't have to confront the fact that when little Johnny brushed his teeth that morning he let the toothpaste explode over the mirror and basin and didn't clean up after himself.

Where the kitchen is the heart of our home, the bathroom is our escape. A bathroom is considered somewhere to disappear into, a place to indulge as you would at a hotel or day spa. More and more people are looking to bathrooms to provide an everyday experience of luxury in their homes. Bathrooms are getting ever larger, taking up a fair chunk of space on a floor plan. Bathrooms can also take an equally huge slice out of your budget whether you're building or renovating, so you want to get it right. All too often, this is where the most expensive mistakes are made.

Where the kitchen is the heart of the home, the bathroom is our escape.

When I first started out in design, the paragon of bathroom luxury was a gigantic spa bath with a number of golden jets furiously pumping away. It didn't matter that the jets were so powerful you could hardly stay in the water, or that the noise of the pump was so brutal you had to get out before you'd even had a chance to wash. A bidet was also a big-ticket item back then, but only the very posh considered installing one. To this day, I still don't really know anyone who uses a bidet, but possibly I'm not moving in the right circles!

Whether it be the tiles, the taps or the rare and forbiddingly expensive type of china used to craft the basin, bathrooms have always had an element of grandeur to them. Today, though, we are more about simple, elegant statements and ensuring that what we put into the bathroom not only looks good now, but will continue to do so for years to come. We have all seen a lot of fads come and go, and people have become a little shy of creat-

Simplicity with white fixtures and tiles is a safe move if you fear taking the leap with a different bathroom look.

Our bathrooms are now considered the most luxurious space in the house.

Oh, how I wish this was my childhood bathroom!

The Showroom: BATH

FREESTANDING

A freestanding bath is one of the most divine fixtures you can put in a bathroom so if luxury is at the top of the list, this is your must-have.

BUILT-IN

A built-in bath can still be given a majestic flourish depending on how it's constructed. The bath pictured features simple white tiles with a 'lip' bench for towels and candles, giving a sense of luxury without using up too much space or going over the top in terms of cost.

TRICK THE EYE

A built-in bath, with one end against a wall and the spout coming up from the floor, looks as extravagant as a freestanding tub.

ing impact in the bathroom. In the backs of their minds they hear a warning voice: 'I must not put in anything but white. That way, it will never date and I won't have wasted my money.'

This is true if you have a rental property or you have one eye on a quick resale, but if you want your bathroom to live and grow with your family, you must consider not only the room's look but its function and soul. The main bathrooms and ensuites in today's homes really need to make a statement to justify taking up all that space. That said, I've also seen many bathrooms that have the undeniable Wow Factor, but then you think, 'So, where do I hang my towel?' or 'There's no way I could fit my hairdryer and cosmetics in here.' The look is integral, of course, but spending a bomb on the tiles and fixtures is a total waste if you end up having to rest your hairdryer on the floor or even in the basin. (Yes, I have seen this happen).

These are the essential points to consider when planning your bathroom/s:
- Bath
- Shower
- Toilet
- Fixtures and fittings
- Storage
- Surfaces
- Ventilation
- Lighting

BATH

A family home of three or more bedrooms must have a bath, even if you don't fancy taking them yourself. Remove it, and you will have really put yourself at a disadvantage if you sell your house at any stage. The main bathroom is the most obvious and common place to put a bath. If you have only one bath and decide to put it in the ensuite, you'll need to make sure it's accessible to the rest of the family.

In an apartment, it doesn't matter so much if it's in either the main bathroom or ensuite, as having a bath at all is considered a luxury. One- and two-bedroom apartments are targeted more at young couples and single people, so baths aren't considered essential.

SHOWER

A shower over the bath is a necessity in a lot of bathrooms, but that doesn't mean it has to look pokey. A frameless half-screen will give a sense of depth to a small area.

A pet hate of mine is shower curtains – why do they always want to float towards you and stick to your body while you're trying to shower? I recommend sidestepping the whole problem by installing a glass screen on the side of your shower. This can be fixed or include a hinge to make it easier to get in and out of the bath.

If you've got the chance to include a separate shower, I say go for it, as it can give a bathroom a

truly lavish feel. It isn't an option for every home, though: firstly, it will come down to space, then to whether there's the access to allow extra plumbing work; and lastly, of course, affordability.

With a walk-in shower, the tiles flow all the way from the main bathroom area to the shower; there isn't the visual 'block' you get with premade shower bases. It can be extremely expensive to put in a walk-in shower when you are renovating, due to the 'fall' that's needed, so that water will flow into the grate. But if it's accommodated right from the start of a build, your costs won't be sky-high. I've heard about people who've initially installed a base because of the costs, thinking they'll be able to put in a walk-in shower further down the track. These people are in for a shock. So, if it's your dream to have a walk-in shower, try to lock it down during the planning stages of a build.

If you have the room, ensure the shower is 1 metre x 1.2 metres (minimum), and then you won't need a shower screen.

TOILET

The big question is, will the toilet go in the bathroom or have its own separate room? If you only have one toilet in the house, it is preferable to have it on its own, possibly with a basin. If you decide to have the toilet in the main bathroom, you'll need to consider if it will make a significant difference to how you live.

When you are undergoing a renovation or a completely new build, I would suggest putting in a minimum of two toilets *if* you are able to. One can sit in the bathroom and the other in a separate room; the latter will be perfect for guests and the rest of the family when someone is having a shower or bath. But as you can see with my client in the case study, two toilets aren't always necessary to seal the deal.

A walk-in shower makes a room seem bigger.

A pre-made shower base is one of the most affordable choices.

BEFORE AND AFTER – CASE STUDY

BEFORE: I worked with some clients who were planning to sell their house a little while down the track – they had brought me in to oversee renovations taking place prior to the sale. At the time, it was a bit tricky balancing the best way to make the space work for the current owners with how this would ultimately affect the home's resale value. The bathroom was dated and the owners knew this would be a major drawback in selling their house. The main debate between the owners and me was over combining the bathroom and separate toilet.

AFTER: In this case, the owners decided on having the only toilet in the main bathroom as it would give them a more spacious bathroom. Subconsciously, the owners ended up having the house *they* really wanted. Rather than being preoccupied with the resale value of their house in the design process, they thought carefully about how they as a family wanted to live in this home. In the end, the clients loved the renovations so much they decided to stay put! It just goes to show that with a bit of tweaking, you might already be living in the house you want. And by combining the two spaces, the owners were able to create a much more luxurious bathroom than they'd previous had.

This house went from a separate bathroom and toilet to combining the two areas, even though it is a one-toilet house.

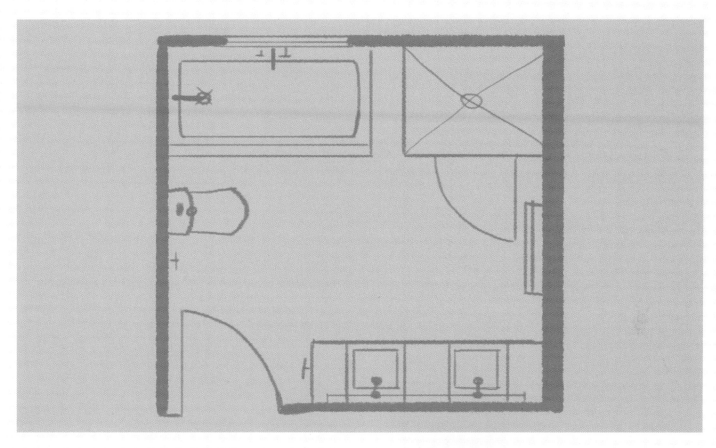

THE PLUMBING

Putting in an extra toilet during a renovation where you are working with the existing space and not adding an extension, means you will definitely have to think about the access to plumbing and how much 'movement' you can get out of your existing floor plan.

A house on stumps allows tradespeople good movement to access the plumbing underneath, and this gives great scope for relocating the bathroom to another part of the house. The costs involved depend on where the sewerage and pipe links are and how far you are moving them from where they were originally. Sometimes when the bathroom is moved to another part of the house, it will be closer to the sewerage links, and so this will be even better than its previous position. But the further away from the main plumbing areas your bathroom moves, the greater your costs.

If your house is on a concrete slab, I can tell you straight out that your options are limited. The toilet will have to stay in its current position. You might have the option of moving the toilet to a different angle, using special plumbing fittings, but other than that you are pretty much stuck with that position unless you want to jackhammer the slab and cause considerable damage and costs.

On the other hand, you *can* move the vanity but this will be restricted without your incurring massive costs. Changing a bathroom on a second storey will also have its restrictions when it comes to wall cavities, in terms of where it lines up with the bottom-storey plumbing and exterior wall access points. I love a plumber who lives by the motto 'never say never' and works with you to get around certain obstacles, but just remember the more you move around plumbing, the more it will cost you.

Updating your bathroom while still keeping everything in the same spot is the ideal way to keep the hidden labour costs down. It also guarantees you are spending the money in the areas you can see: the fixtures, fittings and surfaces.

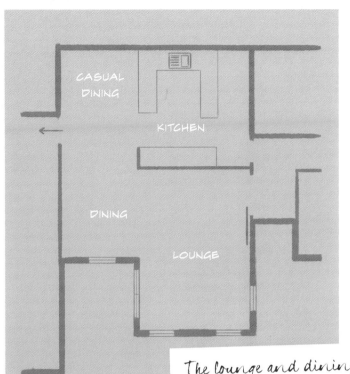

CASUAL
DINING

KITCHEN

DINING

LOUNGE

The lounge and dining room were turned
into a luxury master bedroom and ensuite.
Existing plumbing in the nearby kitchen made
it easy to connect the plumbing, and the raised
timber floor meant access for the sewage.

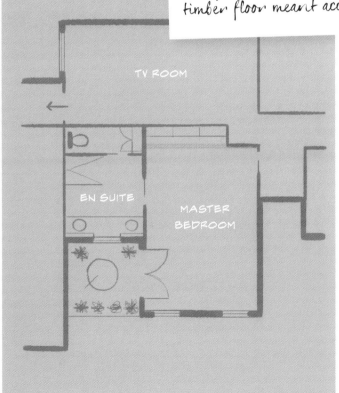

TV ROOM

EN SUITE

MASTER
BEDROOM

The Showroom: BASINS

This is where you can blow a lot of money – it's so easy to get carried away! If you are working to a budget but still want to create an impact, use a couple of key pieces rather than going crazy with everything.

Above-, under-bench or fixed bowls: the choice is endless. For quite a while the above-bench bowl was de rigueur, but now the streamlined look is gaining popularity and the under-bench basin is making a come-back.

BOWL

These round organic-shaped bowls are the main feature of the vanity area. The client splashed out on the bowls and taps, but kept to a minimal look with the vanity.

UNDER-BENCH

Under-bench basins aren't the cheapest option, but even though they're not the stand-out feature here, the lines of the rectangular bowls give the vanity a strong look.

As a fair amount of money was spent on the bowls, the original taps were reused but still matched the deco look the client was going for.

The Showroom: TAPS

BASIN SET

This basin set adds to the romantic look of the bathroom. If a modern pillar tap had been used, it would have looked out of place.

WALL TAP

The reach of the spout needs to be considered when you have an above-bench bowl so make sure you get the length measurements before ordering.

PILLAR TAP

A pillar tap makes a statement and can overshadow the basin so make sure you select one that suits the bowl.

Chunky square bowls with square-edged pillar taps have a commanding presence.

If you want to give your bathroom a fresh look without going over the top, just changing the fittings will give the room an instant lift with minimum costs.

RAIN SHOWER

Having a rain shower is like being able to take a shower in the open air every day. If you can put one in, do it! The plumbing for it needs to travel up the internal wall and into the ceiling so the plumbing costs will be greater than traditional wall-top assemblies and shower roses.

DOUBLE SHOWER

A double shower fitting gives you the ability to have a static shower, but turn the second shower off and you can have a closer, more concentrated water flow. These heads can include massage and jet settings to give a therapeutic shower experience.

TOWEL RAIL

The humble towel rail is either completely forgotten about or else turned into a major feature. Always think about how you shower and where you would ideally access your towels. Having a rail right next to the shower isn't always possible but you can add a hook near the shower. If you're a 'think ahead' sort of person, grabbing the towel as you walk in the bathroom and throwing it over the shower recess works just as well!

A simple double towel rail is functional as it gives room for the towels to dry and keeps them all in one spot. A towel rail can be as big or as small as you like. These separate rails are stacked in rows to create a 'tower' on the wall. A heated towel rail is a great luxury addition. Nothing beats a heated towel to wrap around your body on a winter's day.

TOWELS

Towels give an instant injection of colour. You can get a different bathroom every week just by changing your towels.

The vanity in this bathroom had not only dated but was completely dysfunctional. The huge mirror may look good but it's just wasted storage space. The single shelf under the basin too easily becomes cluttered.

BEFORE

STORAGE

Make this your mantra now: 'You can never have enough storage!' Do not compromise your bathroom's function by neglecting to put in enough storage for all the things you need. Account for toiletries, perfumes, hairdryer, makeup, shaving equipment and then, if you can, the backup supplies of shampoo and toilet paper.

There are other functions to consider too. Do you need to have a spot for the bathroom scales so you don't stub your toe on them every day? What about room for extra mirrors so you can see the back of your hair? Or even a shaving mirror?

The best use of storage for your bathroom is right in front of you in the form of the mirrored cabinet. It's quite brilliant, really, the way it doubles up in terms of its functions: in it, you get to see your gorgeous self getting ready *and* it hides all your lotions and potions. Reserve the cabinets underneath for larger items.

The basin's plumbing will always determine what you can and can't keep underneath storage-wise, and that's why it's important to use as much wall space as possible. If you're able to get a set of drawers built into the cabinet, that's even better, as then you can put in dividers and spacers for your makeup and all the little bits and pieces that float around in the bathroom.

AFTER

BASKETS AND TRAYS

Use baskets and trays to keep organised.

DRAWER DIVIDERS

Using little trays and dividers inside drawers will stop things from sliding around.

SHELVING

Open shelving gives a sense of space to the room. The majority of the storage here comes in the form of cabinet shelving, and the open shelves are used for spare towels.

CABINETS

These streamlined cabinets sit within the cavity wall, providing much-needed storage in a busy family's bathroom. The vanity combines the practicality of the drawers and a sense of space that comes with open shelving.

Use every little bit of space you have. Even that area next to the toilet might fit a cabinet! It's a great space to hold extra toilet rolls, bathroom scales and any other items that aren't needed on a regular basis.

STORAGE WALL

Look at the different ways you can add storage: this wall divider was put in to give privacy for the toilet, but I never like to let a wall space go underutilised. It provides the perfect spot to hide the hairdryer and other bulky items. If you have a long toilet room look at adding a storage wall at one end.

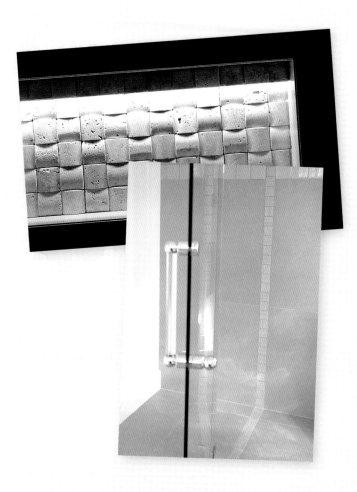

TEXTURES

A simple contrast, such as with these mosaic tiles on the shower shelf against the basin splashback, gives this room extra texture and makes a muted statement when in the same tones as the rest of the room.

FEATURE TILES

Here is clever use of a feature tile that goes from the shower all the way down to the floor and keeps going. This adds contrast in an individual way that won't date.

Stray from the traditional and look at putting the feature tiles on the outside of the shower.

NEUTRAL COLOURS

Varying shades of neutral colours in the tiles creates a warm and earthy experience in the bathroom.

GLASS

The owner of this bathroom has no fear, obviously. Digitally printed glass creates a bold statement; just try to stop yourself from singing along as you shower!

SURFACES

These are the big-ticket permanent items. The cost of what you decide to put on your walls, floors and benchtops won't stop with the material you buy; you'll also need to think of labour costs involved in repairing them. On top of that, consider how much it'll cost to remove them if you don't get the decision right in the first place. You can start to see why people get stressed about making these sorts of choices, and why white and off-white are so popular – they seem to be the safest bet.

I have nothing against white on white, but I find a lot of bathrooms tend to look lifeless and clinical if there isn't a point of difference, such as layers of contrasting colours, tones or textures. If you want a clean and simple look, with the floor and wall tiles exactly the same, that's fine, but pick a tile that has a slight grain or surface texture to it. This will mean that it doesn't look like a big white flat 'board' is sitting on top of your floor and walls. This is where you'll need to create interest through your vanity and walls to save the bathroom from looking like a hospital room.

For a bold look, choose either a benchtop that's white with a grain detail and go with a contrast colour in the cabinetry, or go for a stand-out colour like a hardwood timber benchtop with white cabinetry.

If you want to take a bolder approach, work with contrast and detail in your tiles. You can do this in a couple of ways.

Having your floor a darker colour than the wall tiles will really define this surface without going overboard. However, if you have a tiny bathroom, don't make the contrast between floor and walls too dramatic, as it will make the room seem even smaller.

Feature tiles and feature walls of tiles are how you can really make your bathroom come alive. The options are endless in creating contrast and points of interest: full walls of texture or colour, a contrast line running the vertical length of the

Contrast creates impact.

The colour contrasts here are subtle. Notice the floor tile 'floating' on the main wall, making it really 'pop' against the lighter-coloured tiles used in the rest of the room.

The 3.6m walls of this ensuite would have dwarfed the room had they been covered in tiles. Instead, the tiles sitting midway up the wall puts the focus on the basin area.

bathroom wall, small nooks or shelves, or you could go the whole way and have full walls of dramatic detail.

Again, this is where you really need to be certain you can live with the look you've chosen. Changing tiles is not as easy as removing wallpaper or applying a new coat of paint, *but* you shouldn't be fearful of making bold choices either: you can make it work.

TILES

Tiles come in a multitude of varying sizes: most common are the 200 mm squares and 100 x 200 mm rectangles that are used in traditional and 'retro' fit-outs. In more modern bathrooms, tiny and

large tiles are used depending on the look that is desired. For dramatic detail, full-scale murals or walls of bold colour can be made using 5-mm mosaic tiles, or you can take the minimal lead with large slabs of ceramic, porcelain or marble in 1-metre squares or using full-wall panels, minimising grout lines.

The choice in size and style in tiles is so vast it can be utterly overwhelming. If you struggle to commit to a certain look but don't want the room to be 'beige and boring', keep the tiles neutral and break out in colour with paint, wallpaper or accessories to build your confidence in trying something different.

PAINT

The big trend at the moment is floor-to-ceiling tiles. There are a few reasons behind its popularity: it makes for a bathroom that's easy to keep clean, it also gives a uniformed look, makes the room look larger, and reduces the amount of mould or mildew. On the downside, this can add thousands of dollars to your bathroom budget, which might mean compromising on the quality of your fittings. It isn't considered a design fault not to take your tiles all the way up the wall, especially if you have very high ceilings.

When you paint your bathroom, it's important you use paint that's going to stand up to steam and moisture. Of course, good ventilation is needed, but the added surface protection to your walls and ceiling through using the right paint will keep your bathroom mould-free.

WALLPAPER

Wallpaper is perfect when you want to make that bold statement but don't want the worry of it being a permanent fixture. In the 1970s and 1980s, most wallpaper used in bathrooms had a very tough vinyl coating to help combat mould and mildew, but it also gave a horrible 'plastic' look to the wallpaper. These days, with better ventilation and fans, bathroom heating and high-quality papers and glues, your selection is limitless.

There are a couple of points to consider, though. Don't put your wallpaper behind any wet areas, like the basin or close to the bath area. And don't use grass papers as they are made of actual reeds and grasses that are porous. These types will soak up the moisture no matter how much ventilation you have, and will eventually go mouldy.

Here, tiles are only used in the wet area. It was a case of keeping the costs down while creating an impact using the feature tiles and the basin area.

This bathroom speaks of high-end glamour. The wallpaper features small glass beads that catch the light. This wallpaper's pattern is big and dramatic, but it's only in the one colour and the pattern is only visible when the beads catch the light.

VENTILATION

Sunlight coming through a window not only brightens up a bathroom and gives it a sense of openness, but can also help with mould issues. Leaving the window open to circulate fresh air and let out steam is another very simple, natural way to control the temperature and airflow in a room. Bathroom ventilation used to be via a basic vent through which air passed into the ceiling or out through an exterior wall. Things have really come along way since then. Modern bathrooms feature electrical vents that draw up the steam into the ceiling cavity; and we have units that ventilate, heat and provide light all in one. With leaps forward in technology, ventilation units have become ever more sleek, silent and multi-functional. Positioning the vent close to the source of the steam will prevent the rest of the room from getting mouldy. Near the shower is ideal.

LIGHTING

Every woman hates bad lighting. The wrong type of lighting can give you bags under your eyes and make you look pasty. The perfect way to be lit is from three sources – in front of you, from the sides and surrounding natural light. Now this is, of course, hard to achieve in the bathroom: most of our windows are near the bath area, and including overhead and side lighting can really interfere with the function of the room. But there are a couple of ways to light a bathroom that won't leave you gasping in horror every time you go to put on your makeup.

Directing lights over the *centre* of the basin means that the side of the light beam hits your face. If the light is directly over your head, it will create those nasty shadows under your eyes.

Indirect light coming from two sides, perhaps from off your mirror or cabinetry, creates a 'soft' lighting effect. The light beams 'cross over' and minimise the harshness of a direct light source.

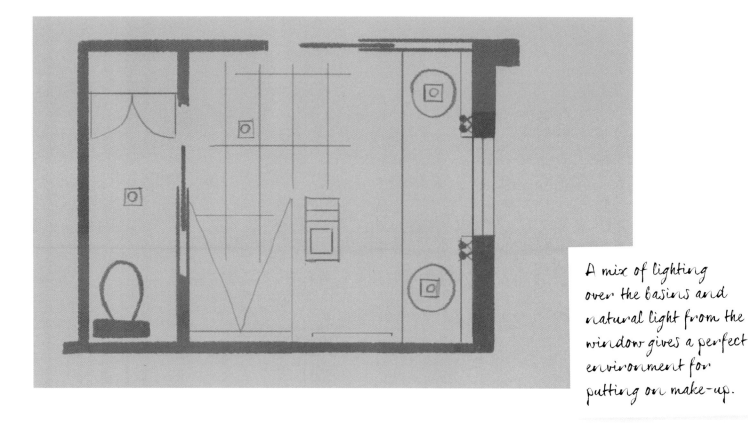

A mix of lighting over the basins and natural light from the window gives a perfect environment for putting on make-up.

Subtle LED lighting is perfect as a night light.

Make sure your light bulbs and tubes emit 'warm' rather than 'cool' light. Cool and warm refer to colour temperature in light bulbs. Lighting is measured on the Kelvin scale: cool colours rate at 4000 K or higher, and give off a blue light, whereas warm colours emit an orange- or red-toned light and sit at around 3000 K. You can see this scale on the label. The cool white light is what gives you that tired and washed-out look.

We spend so much money on our bathrooms to create a luxurious feel, going just that little step further with clever lighting makes sense.

Choosing the right sort of lighting can create mood and add layers and depth to the bathroom's atmosphere. A small LED strip in this alcove gives an extra dimension to the room. This type of lighting not only adds mood but can double up as a night-light for kids so they don't have to worry about walking into the bathroom in the dark. LEDs are efficient and cheap; they don't give off any heat and can last up to ten years before needing to be replaced.

The main bathroom is the place to keep the look and layout simple as this is a space that needs to accommodate the whole family and guests. En-suites are where you get the opportunity to express your individuality and style. Bathroom surfaces are permanent so it is always best to select finishes that reflect your fundamental style preferences, rather than ones dictated by trends that may result in your bathroom dating quickly.

Hidden lighting behind the mirrored cabinets creates a 'halo' feature visually, but also functions as soft light on the face.

An open window is the easiest way to direct steam out of the bathroom, and it costs you nothing!

The greatest thing about using these three-in-one fixtures is it minimises the fittings on the ceiling, keeping it simple and uncrowded.

And if you don't care about make-up, as with the boys who use this bathroom, you can use lights as a feature. The blue light inside the basin lends a nightclub feel to the space.

Small light shades not only look great in a bathroom but give the face a soft glow.

RULES ROUND-UP

- Determine who will use the room on a daily basis and what their immediate storage needs are.

- Will you have a separate toilet or include it in the main bathroom?

- Create interest and contrast with your floor and wall tiles.

- Plan your lighting and ventilation at the same time as your plumbing layout.

- Tapware is just as important as your surfaces, so take time in your selection.

- A family home must have a bath, especially when it comes to selling.

- Storage, storage and storage.

- Did I mention storage?

- For flexibility of look, only tile in wet areas, so that you can easily change wall colour or add wallpaper later.

- Create luxury by putting texture in your tiles and surfaces.

- Look at hidden lighting to add another dimension to the room.

BEDROOM
Who you really are

BEDROOM

I believe our bedrooms express who we are. Our living areas are about the whole family spending time together and making friends feel welcome. A bedroom, however, is our haven, the place we wake up in the morning and so it should help us to energise for the day ahead. It is also where we rest our tired bodies and overactive brains, so our bedrooms should also be conducive to lulling us to sleep.

This is the place to escape work, the kids, and give you a chance to focus on you. My bedroom is one of my favourite rooms and I have always made a big deal of it in every house I have lived. I suppose it comes down to the fact that while I was growing up, my bedroom always seemed to symbolise freedom of expression: as a kid I was allowed to do what ever I wanted to my bedroom, as long as I physically did it and paid for it. As you can imagine, it was all done in a 'hack' way. Even so, I have always loved how a bedroom can be whatever you want it to after you close the door: it is the perfect way to get away from the stress of everyday life.

If you have a partner, there will have to be compromises, and it is important that both people have their say. Cue my husband asking, 'Where was my say?' But he doesn't place as much importance on the bedroom as I do – *and* he says he loves the way our bedroom looks (that's what he tells me anyway).

All the bedrooms in your home – whether they are a master wing or a bedroom that is a kids' play room by day or a bedroom-cum-office – need to be planned right from the start. Don't become fixated on the pattern of the doona (that is part of deciding your colours and textures) and try to build your room around that; the first thing is to get the mechanics right so no one goes bump in the night.

The design principles and ideas in this chapter work for all bedrooms in the house, no matter their size or shape.

LAYOUT

When you are trying to find the best place for the bed, your main obstacles are the door, wardrobe and window. Sometimes there is more than one window and more often than not you're left with only the one option as to where to put your bed.

BEDROOM LAYOUTS

In this bedroom we have two options as to where to place the bed: on the wall by the door or on the wall to the right of the door. Either will work, but the choice comes down to the size of the room and bed.

IDEAL LAYOUT

This layout not only works functionally, but when you walk into the room, you notice the bed, artwork and colours rather than looking straight at the large functional chest of drawers to the side. Even though the window is prominent, it isn't a big feature; the dramatic combination of the bed's position and how it is dressed captures your attention. Even though there is a bold orange wall, having it on the side (and so in your peripheral vision) means it isn't overbearing.

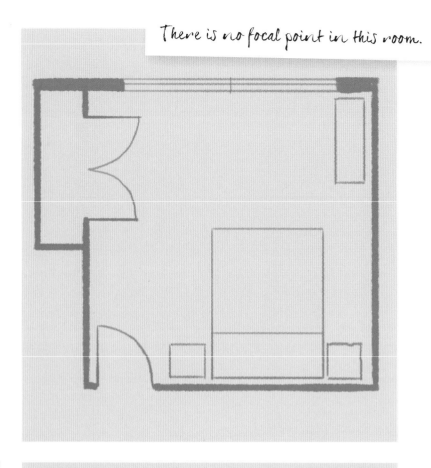

There is no focal point in this room.

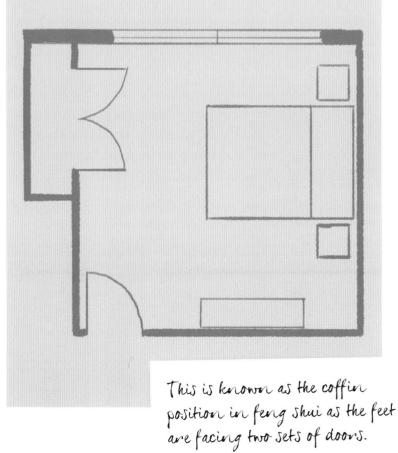

This is known as the coffin position in feng shui as the feet are facing two sets of doors.

You notice the feature artwork
as soon as you walk in.

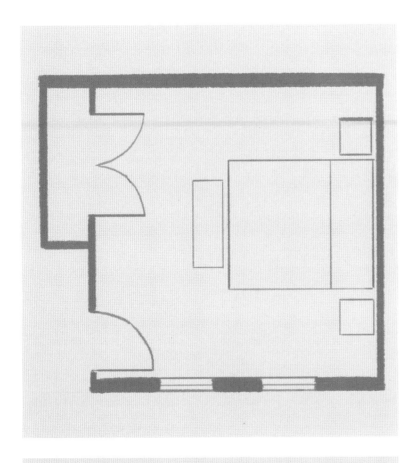

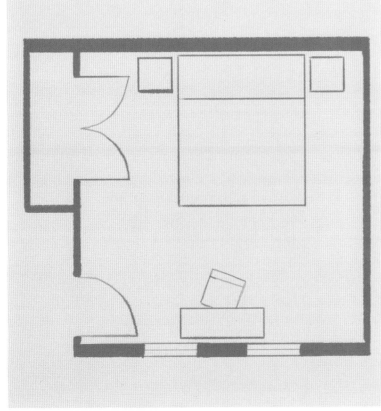

This bedroom is the same size as the previous room, but the layout is quite different because of the positioning of the windows and doors.

VIEW FROM YOUR BED

The bed also works on the wall opposite the entry, giving access to both sides of the bed and good movement around the room and bed opposite the door isn't always the ideal placement, even though it fits space-wise.

In feng shui this is also known as the 'coffin position', as it replicates how are we are placed in a coffin feet first. In feng shui, doors are known as connectors, as opposed to western design where we look at them as barriers. In feng shui, a door is thought to 'pull' energy from one room to the next, and the direction your feet are pointing is important. Here, your energy is escaping out the door as you sleep. To combat this, you must create a barrier between you and the door. This can be simply done with a foot end to your bed, a foot-stool or chair. The door in question can also refer to that of an open walk-in wardrobe.

I find it more about wanting to avoid a 'boring' view to wake up to each morning. If the bed is facing a door or wardrobe, it's not a very inspiring start to the day. If you place the bed opposite the window, you get to wake up to a view everyday. If you have a bad view, make it a priority to get standout window treatments – having a great view to wake up to is vital.

In terms of the layout of your room, it is important to get the right energy and feel. As with all other bedrooms in the house, it is important to have a focal point when you first walk in the room.

Here are some ideas of focal points:
• Outside view
• Window treatment
• Bedhead
• Linen
• Artwork

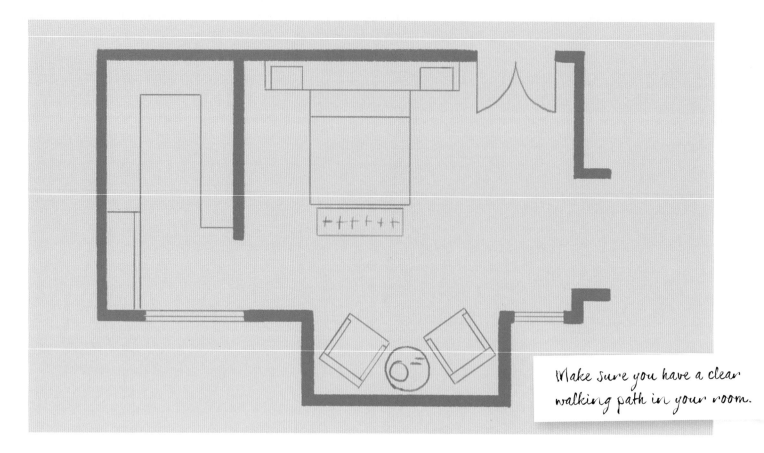

Make sure you have a clear walking path in your room.

THE BASICS

It is always good to have a reference guide when it comes to bed sizes, so work with a tape measure to plan out your space.

- Single: 920 mm x 187 mm
- King single: 1060 mm x 2030 mm
- Double: 1370 mm x 1870 mm
- Queen: 1530 mm x 2020 mm
- King: 183 mm x 2030 mm
- Bedside table: 450 mm x 450 mm, 500 mm x 500 mm
- Foot stool: 300–400 mm x 1500 mm
- Decorator chair: 600 mm x 700–800 mm (you can get larger, but start with a medium size. If this is too big, go for a 'dresser chair', which is more like a dining chair).

Before you go to the shops, map out your bedroom (as you did in your living area), so you know exactly how much space you have to work with. A king bed may be the dream but if you have to climb into the bed from the end or the other side, I guarantee you are going to hate living with it.

Ideally, have a minimum of 700 mm between the wall and the bed for ease of not only getting in and out but for making the bed. It is easy to overlook the simple daily practicalities of your bedroom when you have your eye on the biggest bed.

Use a minimum 800 mm measurement as a guide for the 'walking line' for the rest of the room. If you allow this minimum space and map it out on the floor, you will have a true sense of what you have to work with. However, if it's only 800 mm between the end of the bed and the door or wardrobe it may feel a little cramped.

A foot stool frames a bed beautifully but can add up to 400 mm to the length of your bed. That will eat into your walking space if you have a small room.

When working out the room plan, you need to consider not only walking into the room but also all the other bedroom actions. Make sure you have a clear pathway from both sides of the bed to the door, to prevent you from stubbing your toe in the dark.

In the room opposite there are three exits – the main door, the opening leading to the walk-in robe and another going to the ensuite. All these walking paths need to be considered and left clear. On top of that, there needs to be enough space for people to walk around the bed, as well as to get in and out of it easily.

This is a big master suite with a lot of furniture and there's enough space to handle it, but even so, the owners had to make sure to measure the main items before adding all the extras, like décor chairs and dressing tables.

No matter the size our bedrooms, there is the bare minimum of items needed.

WARDROBES

From walk-in robe to a freestanding cupboard, you need to know what you have to accommodate – but don't let the wardrobe take over the room. I hear gasps of horror from the women of the world, but hear me out: work with the space you have and then see what alternatives are needed for the overflow. Extra shoes and clothes can be stored in spare rooms, or under the stairs, and seasonal wear, such as jumpers and jackets, can be boxed and stored somewhere up high.

Organisation in the bedroom is high on the priority list for creating a restful space. Clutter causes chaos. As this is the place to chill out at the end of the day, it is important to look at how you keep control of any extraneous items in the bedroom. I highly recommend reading books on how to get organised or else getting in a professional organiser to help you solve storage issues in your wardrobe. *From Stuffed to Sorted: Your Essential Guide to Organising, Room by Room* by

MaryAnne Bennie and any books by Peter Walsh will arm you with great skills to get not only your wardrobe sorted but any problem drawers as well. Even go that step further with a stylist, as they will be able to help you get rid of a lot of those shirts you haven't worn since 1994, and make the clothes you do wear work better for you. We wear on average only 20–30 per cent of the clothes in our wardrobe on a regular basis. A good clean-out might surprise you, and reduce the amount of stuff in your wardrobe.

TIP: Freestanding wardrobes with doors need to be a minimum of 600 mm deep so your hangers have enough clearance to sit properly. Wardrobes with sliding doors need to be 700 mm deep to allow for the sliding-door track.

I have left out one major wardrobe type: the floor robe. You know what I'm talking about; it's what happens when you are always in a mad rush, and can't be bothered hanging up the clothes you've pulled out while looking for that one perfect outfit. You say you will clear it up later… in the month?

The Showroom: WARDROBES

WALK-IN WARDROBE

High-end glamour – yes, this is the wardrobe we've all dreamt of. Not everyone will be lucky enough to have a wardrobe as luxe as this, but notice how it is organised to within an inch of its life. Shoes are sectioned into boots, high heels and flats. Shirts, skirts and jackets are given their own sections so getting dressed is easy and not a drama.

DO AWAY WITH DOORS

Think of simple solutions to make your wardrobe fit in with the décor of your room. Not putting doors on the wardrobe and using a stacker blind gives an elegant feel to the room.

FEATURE THE ROOM

Make a statement. This bedroom has a great feature in the form of the window so the wardrobe was designed to pick up on the art-deco lines in its doors. As the room had concrete walls and ceiling, getting extra lighting was difficult. Including lighting in the structure of the wardrobe gave much needed light to the room without having an exposed electrical conduit.

MIRRORED WARDROBE

Mirrored doors are superb. Apart from being a full-length mirror for dressing, they reflect light in a dull room and create the illusion of space. Drawers hidden behind sliding doors give a streamlined look to the bedroom when the door is closed.

    If you have the room, use your shoes or bags as a feature. After all, you've paid enough for them!

CASE STUDY – A STANDARD SHELF AND ROD DOES NOT A WARDROBE MAKE!

When the clients first moved into their new home all that was installed was the customary single rod and one shelf that is included in a basic 'display home' package build. It was important to increase the storage and hanging space, without the option of a large footprint to the wardrobe.

Raising the height of the shelf and creating hanging spaces literally means doubling the space. There is a section at the end for long dresses and shoe shelves, and on the top are boxes for excess storage. The boxes and shelves are in the same colour to streamline the look, while keeping the focus on the clothes.

This wardrobe has used all available vertical space for the client to fit essential clothing for day-to-day living.

BEDSIDE TABLES

Clothes aren't the only personal items you'll need to find a place for in your bedroom. If you think of all the extras you have in there, you might start to feel a little overwhelmed. I'm all for the trend of stools or small tables in the bedroom – they do look amazing – but if you lack space or you're not a very organised person, this can be a disaster.

From day one of setting up your bedroom, think about what you want directly next you as you lie in bed. Do you like to have a glass of water there, a radio or a charger for the phone? Then there are lamps, a book or even a stack of books for reading at night.

UNDER THE BED

The beauty of a slat bed is all that extra room you gain underneath. It's the perfect place to store a spare mattress for when the kids' friends sleep over, drawers to hold seasonal shoes and clothes, or even to hide away those gym items that make you feel guilty for not using them more often.

If your room is on the small side and you lack storage in the bedroom, under the bed should be number one on the list of your planning solutions.

OTHER OPTIONS

An ottoman or foot stool is an elegant piece to sit at the end of the bed, but you can go that step further and get extra depth to it by including a lift-up lid to accommodate extra storage. This can be great if you want to keep your bedside table clutter-free.

A chest is a decorative piece that can be perfect for storing winter/summer clothes that are put away seasonally. This will give you more room in the wardrobe.

TIP: Watch out for antique chests, as they can sometimes emit a musty smell. Combat this with dried clove balls, dried orange peel or cedar balls, and wrap your clothes in acid-free tissue paper.

A cluttered bedside not only looks messy but creates negative energy right where your head rests.

FUNCTION

This bedside not only accommodates the basics of a lamp and a phone but also an 'intimates' drawer, a small library and a bowl to drop earrings and jewellery into before you go to sleep.

STYLE

Bedside tables are highly visible pieces of furniture so be conscious of the style you want to achieve and carry it through in these pieces.

STATEMENT

Your bedside tables don't always have to be a matching pair. The heaviness of the timber, leather and dark colours here is given a slightly more casual feel by altering the heights of the tables and lamps.

LIGHTING

I can imagine some people think of lighting as an accessory, nothing much more than the bedside lamps. As in all rooms, however, lighting is essential in a practical, functional sense and for creating mood, if you know what I mean. Look at your lighting in the bedroom for the basics: the traffic flow, where you need to walk, and the main tasks, such as getting dressed. Unless you like to be blinded in your bed, don't have your light fitting on the ceiling over the bed near the pillows.

For mood and indirect lighting you can't go past candles. This can, of course, be dangerous so opt for LED flameless candles. You can even set these on a timer so they go on at the same time you go to bed and turn themselves off after you've fallen asleep.

BEAUTIFYING

There are so many ways you can add features to a bedroom, but be careful when it comes to how much. Our bedrooms tend to be the smallest living spaces in the house; going over the top in your decorating can be quite suffocating. If your windows and window treatments aren't your feature, decide what it is you want to stand out in your bedroom. The obvious item is the bed but if you don't see the bed as soon as you walk into the room, then the rest of the space could seem a little flat and boring. Make sure you have a few other interesting features to capture the eye.

Our bedrooms tend to be the smallest living spaces in the house; going over the top in your decorating can be quite suffocating.

Flameless candles are perfect to use as a night-light if your kids are afraid of the dark.

Do you hate the morning light streaming in or are you happy with a soft glow waking you up of a morning? For full block-out, curtains are the only solution. A dense fabric with a high-grade block-out lining the curtain will ensure the sunshine's kept at bay, but to get maximum darkness take the curtain to the edge of the wall and as close as possible up to the ceiling. A pelmet with a fixed top will give you the ultimate block-out but it's not really in style at the moment, and can create too much bulk to an interior, especially if you have low ceilings.

CURTAINS

Fabrics in curtains and roman blinds add a sense of warmth to a room as the texture in the fabric is an insulator. If you select a fabric with a low-sheen finish, it will also look a lot warmer. If your bedroom faces the afternoon sun, your window treatments are just as important for controlling the temperature in the room.

These curtains not only go to the ceiling but sit 100 mm past the window frame. This gives less chance for natural light to 'bleed' into the room.

SHUTTERS

Shutters won't completely block out the sun but as they are sealed around the window, this reduces light. Depending on the way you angle the blade, you can control how much light you let in. Tilt the blades up and the light is directed to the ceiling and not onto the floor. This directs the light away from the bed and makes the light seem less intrusive.

DUAL BLINDS

Dual blinds are perfect for privacy and blocking out some light, but don't give you the ultimate block-out in a bedroom. Not all blinds can be hung internally in the frame of the window, so when it is on the outside there is quite a bit of area for the light to splay onto the wall even when fully down.

ROMAN BLINDS

Roman blinds can give you a good level of block-out if you make sure the blinds go 70–100 mm past the window frame. Not all windows have this amount of room to play with, but the further you go away from the glassed area the best chance you have of trapping the light behind the blind.

PAINT AND WALLPAPER

Using paint colours and wallpaper are an easy way to add interest to a room that has no obvious architectural features or focal points.

Wallpaper captures you as soon as you walk in the room. Wallpaper is perfect for adding colour and interest to a bedroom scheme without having to rely on artwork or curtains to create the room's atmosphere. Wallpaper can be used on all walls or as a feature on one main wall. A feature works well behind the bed in place of a decorative headboard, or put one behind any open shelving you might have or above a tallboy to make a small feature without going over the top. I recommend (in fact, *highly* recommend) getting the professionals in to hang wallpaper –

it's a big job, from wall preparation, using glues and taking into account the different types of papers and their idiosyncrasies. Always get your wallpaper hanger to work out how many rolls needed for a wall because the size of the pattern has an effect. Allowing enough to match up the pattern means the same wall could take two or four rolls. Generally, the bigger the pattern, the more wallpaper required.

After their overuse in the 1990s, feature walls have left us feeling a bit scared of them, but don't let that stop you from putting one in your bedroom. It is the perfect addition in a simple room to add 'oomph' to a bedroom. Use it as an inspiration for colours in your bed linen.

The horizontal stripes lead your eye to the bed on the left-hand side and the feature artwork to the right. The slight shimmer in the silver stripe catches in different lights and gives a delicate feel to the hard line of the stripes.

BED LINEN

Plain, patterned and solid-coloured bed linen can give your room a totally new look every time you do the washing. Strong colours and patterns in a room means your bed will be the statement piece, so make sure this is where you want the focus to be.

This isn't just the doona we are talking about but the sheets, pillowcases, decorator cushions and throws. I have heard men out there complain it takes them twenty minutes to get into bed by the time they fight through the cushions and put the throw back properly – and longer in the morning if they are forced to make the bed. A slight exaggeration, I am sure. That said, you can go overboard with your bed accessories. When you are selling your home and want to add lots and lots of colour then five, even seven, cushions (yes, I love cushions!) on a bed is brilliant. But if you find negotiating that many cushions each night leaves you angry, then simplify it. After all, we are told never to go to bed angry!

BEDHEADS

There are quite a few options to framing your bed and they can be governed by the shape of your bed frame. A simple bed and base give you total flexibility on how you dress your room. You can use a fabric bedhead, artwork, hung fabrics, even slabs of timber… the list is only limited by your imagination. With a fixed bed frame, you are locked into the look but you can eventually change that by keeping the mattress and getting a new base. We tend to hang onto a look in our bedroom for around ten years and the bed is what governs it, so make sure when you are purchasing a bedhead or fixed bed frame you are fairly certain that you're going to love it for a long time.

You can use a fabric bedhead, artwork, hung fabrics, even slabs of timber … the list is only limited by your imagination.

DRESSING TABLES

If you have the room for it, there is nothing more decadent than a dressing table. A place to sit and get ready for the day or evening ahead, it is like taking a moment not only to pamper yourself but sit with your thoughts – what an indulgence! A dressing table can also double as an elegant writing desk, with the added bonus of extra storage.

DECORATIVE FURNITURE

An extra piece of furniture in the bedroom not only looks great but can be used in many practical ways. A bed is around 550–700 mm high, so sitting on it to put your shoes on can be a bit awkward (especially if you are height-challenged like I am).

A gorgeous chair in the bedroom can be just the remedy. You can drape your outfit for the next day over the top with shoes ready to step into nearby. It can become a spot to curl up in to read a book as you escape from the rest of the family, especially as lying on the bed during the day can be easily spoilt by the lazy-guilt factor. It can also be the extra chair that comes out when you've got guests.

MULTIPURPOSE BEDROOMS

I always hear the arguments about to TV or not TV, and whether it's okay to have laptops or desks in the bedroom. The case against being that these activities will stimulate the brain at a time when you should be switching off to go to sleep. I am not here to preach to you either way, but my main tip is that if you do have a desk or TV in there, don't make it a feature of the room. It is to be secondary to what is meant to be going on: getting dressed/undressed, taking time out and sleeping well.

Many kids' rooms have built-in desks for their school study right from primary up to university, and that is practical. It is important to make the study area feel part of the bedroom so it isn't singled out as an odd piece in the room.

The Showroom: BED LINEN

BALANCE

There is no hiding that the girl who lives in this room loves pink, and that it's a room that is all about glitz and glamour. This is exactly what I mean about creating an individual look in a room — it's really all about you. The rest of the room is quite understated to give the bold patterns and colour room to breathe.

CLASSIC

Simple crisp white linen is a perfect base to create any look you're after. The black edging of the pillows and doona give strength to the look and by not adding any decorator cushions or colour, the room has a classic simplicity to it.

COLOUR

If you are afraid of bold colours in the linen, keep the sheets and doona simple and add splashes of colour in the throw and cushions.

MIRRORED BEDHEAD

Even though this bedhead with its mirrored edging is dramatic, the design is simple, elegant and will remain timeless. To change the look it is a simple case of just changing the linen and cushions.

CAST IRON BEDFRAME

An old iron bed can make you think you can only have an old-style room. However, powder-coating the frame in black gives a new life to this antique bed. Having the same black on the wall and bedside tables means they have a link to each other: the frame almost disappears and avoids being the standout feature most of these beds tend to be.

FABRIC BEDHEAD

A fabric bedhead attached to the wall gives the room flexibility to change in the future. However, in this instance, the bedhead is part of the whole look of the interior so if the bedhead were to change, it may not give the bedroom the same elegant look it has now.

ARTWORK BEDHEAD

Use artwork as a bedhead. If it is flexibility in terms of changing your look that drives you, putting a few nails in the wall every now again shouldn't concern you. Large recycled doors give a sturdiness to the bedroom interior and the colour of the timber gives inspiration for the bed linen. Change the heavy timber to a delicate kimono and you create a more subtle and peaceful feel in the room. Using Euro pillows for your bed is a simple way to add height to your bed without going 'over the top' in the look.

The Showroom: DRESSING TABLES

JUST FOR FUN

A dressing table doesn't have to be a fully practical piece of furniture: it can also be a place to display perfume bottles and your favourite pieces of jewellery.

PRACTICAL

A drawer with an insert gives the practicality of extra space without the bulk of seeing all the drawers on the outside.

A PLACE TO GET READY

A mirror is the perfect accessory for a dressing table. Having all your jewellery in the one spot means it is not only a beautiful place to get ready but it's easy to lay your jewellery out at the end of the night.

CHAIRS

This elegant upholstered chair fits beautifully in the bedroom but is actually a dining chair from another room. The dining room on a daily basis can only hold six chairs comfortably, but the owner needed two extra chairs so one is used in the bedroom while the other is used as an office chair.

Glam up a practical chair with items from your wardrobe.

FOOTSTOOL

This apartment wasn't large but it did have a decent-sized bedroom. This foot stool is not only handy for sitting on but would look great covered with a bag and the spoils of a shopping trip. Having bags and clothes resting or hanging on a piece of furniture can look decorative and elegant in a room, compared to when they're strewn on the floor.

SETTING

You need to have a retreat area in your bedroom to accommodate a feature like this. It may seem over the top but it is still highly functional: a reading lamp beside the chair, a table to the side for any drinks or snacks as you relax, and an ottoman to rest your feet on while reading. The ottoman has a hard top with a covering of Dacron; this gives it a structure that will support being sat on or using it to rest a tray on without it becoming unstable.

KIDS' ROOMS

When you have a single bed it indicates a kid's or teenager's room, and these are definitely the rooms to have fun with. I think the décor of kids' rooms needs to undergo at least four different changes over the course of childhood.

NURSERY: Mum and Dad have control.
TODDLER, AGED TWO—FIVE: Mum and Dad still have control. As the kids become more active, it is time to make the room child-proof; this is also when you shift from a nursery cot to a bed. The bedroom becomes a play room as much as a place to sleep. It is important for a child's development that this room be highly practical. This is where they learn to chose their own clothes, put them away and put them in the laundry basket. Here is where they put their toys away, amuse themselves during quiet time, listen to books being read and learn to read them.

STARTING SCHOOL, AGED FIVE—TEN: This is the time to work as a team. When your kids start school, they are 'big kids' now. They are grown up in their eyes and it is time for them to also make the decisions in their rooms. What I suggest is waiting for them to suggest that they want to make a change (and this may not be until they are age seven or so); that way they can feel ownership. When a child gains ownership of their room, it is theirs and this gives them a good start in taking care of what they 'own'.

Once they want to make changes, treat it as a project to talk about first: their ideas of a slide coming through the ceiling into a pit of jelly isn't really going to happen – *or is it?* Once you move from fantasy to things that you *can* change, work with them: ask what they want, and why. If it isn't practical, let them know why and suggest something else. Let them know the things you can and can't afford and hopefully compromise.

When it's time to buy everything, do it together. When you have to build things or paint the walls, let them help you. At this age, it is possibly the last time they will give you a hand in getting their room ready so you may as well make the most of it!

AGED TEN AND ONWARDS: Let them go. Yes, control freaks look away. This is their room; it is about them expressing their personality through this space. Now, I'm not talking about letting them knock down walls or rip up the floorboards or anything, but do let them select their paint, put posters on the walls, bring in the musical instruments, paint the ceiling black.

The compromise is they'll still have to do all the basics: putting things away, cleaning up afterwards, and so on, but letting them express themselves simply by selecting the doona cover and paint colour means it is their own little piece of nirvana.

RULES ROUND-UP

- What are your obstacles when planning? Door, window, wardrobe? Map the room so you have a clear space to walk around and can easily get in and out of bed.

- Have a focal point – a good view when you walk in the room will stimulate you.

- Don't clutter the room with unnecessary furniture.

- Your wardrobe should work hard for every square centimetre of space so get it organised.

- Lighting is your friend in the bedroom so use mood lighting as well as task lighting.

- Use a window treatment that suits your type of sleeping: heavy or light.

- Buy the best linen you can afford to get a luxurious feeling against your skin every morning and night.

- If you have to have a desk in your bedroom, make it work with the bedroom furniture rather than looking like it's part of an office.

HOME OFFICE

Working from home

HOME OFFICE

Most of us can't help but bring our work home with us now and then, but up until recently having an allocated space just for the home office wasn't featured in designs. It was considered more of a token room for show than a proper functional space. With our portable work lives, a home business is not frowned upon anymore and working from home is an added incentive in the corporate world. A large study is perfect to keep the line between home and work distinct, and when organised properly it can not only be functional but inviting.

An 'office' can be a room, a desk in the bedroom, part of your lounge room, or even at the kitchen bench as you hold conference calls while wiping Vegemite off your kids' faces. Our work and office life is more flexible and transient than ever before so making our working roles part of our home life without it taking over can be a major challenge.

No matter what part of the house the home office is in, storage is the key to making it work. On the other hand, the ability to keep the desk or bench clear is an ongoing challenge. There are days when my desk resembles a search and rescue mission, as I need access to paint samples, fabrics, tiles and catalogues all at the same time. I not only need the desk as a working space but as an extra table to keep reference items for anything up to a week.

BEDROOM

For both adults and kids alike, sometimes we have no choice but to use the bedroom as a site for work. There are ways, however, to keep clutter to a minimum and maintain the serene, peaceful atmosphere of the bedroom – so that you don't wake up at 3 a.m. after having a nightmare about that report!

When you're working from home, make the office area as visually pleasing as possible, so you don't end up with a sterile corner in a room.

VISUAL SIMPLICITY

Not only is this a big room, every space inside and out, including cupboards or drawers is organised to within an inch of its life. The client knew exactly what she wanted to store and how much extra space she would need in the future. The room was not only to function smoothly but look great, as the door is always open to the front hallway. This office stores all the family's photo albums, materials for projects, study and reference books while also being an office away from the main business office.

TEXTURAL BREAK

A large wall of storage can be confronting, so to break up the sheer size of the doors and room, the veneer grain was arranged in a vertical and horizontal pattern. To break up the solid look of timber, a workspace was integrated with a shellac splashback as a feature.

ATTENTION TO DETAIL

The elegant desk has dramatic chrome legs and the box-type top has beautiful slim-line drawers to hold all the small bits and pieces that clutter up a desk. The desk is set up on a daily basis with two chairs, but is deep enough at 1200 mm, to be able to seat four people at any time.

FOCAL POINT

Sometimes you have to sacrifice a main living area or bedroom to make that home business work. In any business, all the tools of the trade need to be at your fingertips, the added challenge is, as it is in a home, that it still needs to be visually pleasing. Keeping all the storage under eye-level and putting the focus on strong artwork gives the room a balance between home and office. Personal touches are always encouraged in a home business and even more so when it is open to the rest of the house.

COMFORT

Ergonomic chairs with lumbar support, wheels, and swivel action help to create a comfortable workspace and put everything easily within arm's reach. The distance between you and the desk, be it against either a wall or storage, needs to be a minimum 900 mm so you have enough room to move in and out of your chair.

There's not always going to be the room to have a dedicated space for an office or study. More and more these days we are catching up on emails or reading that brief in among the hubbub of family life. The kitchen or the lounge room will often double up as a place of work or study, and these spaces have to be flexible enough to accommodate.

THE WORKING KITCHEN

With some planning, this kitchen has become a mini business hub. A hidden powerpoint for the phones to charge is great, but go down a drawer further and an extra set of power points charges the printer. This is the perfect spot for talking business and printing out notes over coffee. Who needs a café?

Clutter is one of the biggest enemies of a kitchen bench, and if you are trying to work at the bench or have the kids do their homework while you cook, small hide-away drawers are essential. The powerpoint on the side of the bench is used for kitchen appliances, like blenders and so on, but it can also be used to power your laptop. A drawer next to it lets you charge a phone without it being knocked off the bench. While the drawer below that allows you to put in the basic office stationery items. That way, only the basics like the laptop and a notebook need to be on the bench.

HIDDEN OFFICE

The cupboards on the underside of the bench show storage for plates but is the perfect depth for folders that not only hold work details but kids' newsletters, rosters, takeaway menus, and so on.

SECRET OFFICE

A big wall of doors has a sense of intrigue to it and the luxurious wall of earthy surfaces like timber, stone and an inviting fireplace hides a flurry of activity going on behind it.

A set of pocket doors slides back to reveal a study nook that holds all the kids need to do their homework. Having a desk in the main living area means the kids don't feel isolated, and in a world where social media rules, it means parents can keep an eye on what the little kids are up to.

GUEST ROOM AND OFFICE

A multifunctional room that's a guest room, reading nook and office means one big relaxing environment. These two desks are positioned perfectly for feng shui, and not having to worry about any walls behind the desk gives ample room to swivel around in the chairs!

A guest room/office is the perfect combination. The sofa bed-couch evokes a relaxing feeling, as it is the first thing you notice when you walk in. Being able to sit at the couch to do research or take a break not only creates an easy-going environment but is a good space to hold meetings if clients come to the house.

As the room is full of hard surfaces with the desk and side table, the plumpness of the ottoman becomes a great place to rest the eyes. It also becomes a practical tool at the end of the day: put your feet up as you pat yourself on the back for how hard you have worked!

UTILISE EVERY PLACE

Hidden storage in the reading nook is perfect to store extra bedding when guests come to visit.

HARMONY

Making the storage cabinets the same colour as the walls helps them disappear and gives an illusion of more space. To take even more focus away from any overhead storage, put in a feature like wallpaper. Highlight it with fixed cabinetry lights, which provide task lighting as well as being decorative.

DECOR CHAIRS

If your desk and storage is in the one spot, you can go for a more decorative chair. If you are sitting at the desk for studying, and other projects, the chair still needs to support your back properly.

HIDE THE CLUTTER

When you have a small room that need a lots of storage or doubles up as a bedroom, put as much as you can behind doors or in drawers to reduce the clutter. Leave the open shelves for decorative items, rather than books and folders. This will give a simple and streamlined look to a small room.

sandman h

BEFORE AND AFTER – CASE STUDY

BEFORE: Creating a total bedroom/study space is about creating balance of work and play.

In this house it was not just about a home office but creating a sleeping/living area as well.

AFTER: A dividing wall was removed to create one big space.

There were so many things to consider for this bedroom, like a wardrobe, bed and lights but also the added needs for an office, equipment, stationery and a desk. A division was necessary so it didn't feel like a 24-hour workroom. This wardrobe became dual function – for clothes and office supplies.

Mirrors are ideal for getting dressed but not always functional for an office. This vinyl chalkboard not only functions for notes but as it sits behind the computer it cuts glare reflecting onto the computer screen.

Every item not only had to look good but also have a function. The bookshelf holds a display that is relevant to the photographer's job and can be used for future reference material. Visually, it creates a break between the office and bed while the fine-tassled curtain acts as a divider without blocking any light or creating a closed-in feel to the room.

RULES ROUND-UP

- If you work from home, doors are rarely closed on the office area, so maximise storage space to keep it clutter free.

- If your home office is a mini-hub in the kitchen, it needs to blend in with its surroundings. Keep mess behind doors and in well-designed drawers.

- Justify the space. Multifunctional rooms like office/bedroom and office/spare room means the room is used more often and is not just wasted space.

- Personalise the area to make working from home enjoyable. Use pictures and items so that it looks more like part of the house than a tacked-on room or an afterthought.

- Lighting is not decorative in the office, so make sure overhead lights and desk lamps work together.

- Chairs need to be functional for long stints of work.

OVER TO YOU ...

You have got to the end, well done! You are now armed with rules that will give you the confidence to design a home that functions around the way you live. Use this book chapter by chapter, room by room, and look at how each space is going to work for you and your family, to make it the best possible home you imagined. Each individual room will work well, and will flow and connect the whole house so it's a great home to live in. I know we all dream of the gorgeous lamp, the perfect couch filled with cushions and having a home that we can proudly invite our friends to, and now you are on the way to achieving that dream. My rules are the foundation to achieving not just a well designed space but a home. Your home.

Enjoy designing your home.

Shaynna

Writing an interior design book has been a dream for such a long time, and to do something as important as this doesn't happen overnight. There are many family, friends and business people who have lifted me personally, spiritually and professionally over the years, and I am truly grateful for the people in my life now and for those who have made their presence felt along the way. To gush about you all personally is a novel of its own, so rather than bore you to tears a list will keep the word and page limit down quite considerably!

So here I go:

Mum & Dad, Wayne & Eileen, Maddison & Davin, Joan & Gerry, Sundae, Brett, Shane & Brenda, Chris & Kate, Jenni & Mark, Ange, Victoria & Todd, Katrina & Simon, Karolina & Atilla, Andy & Michael, Lauren, Elisha & Daniel, Tracy, Samara, Ben & Nikki, Bardi & Michael, Carolyn, Donna, MaryAnne, Yvonne, Angie, Frances, Belinda, Barbara, Jo, Daniel, Mitchell, Vanessa, Alan W, Amy & Pete, Sonia, Geoff, Matt, Tim, Andrew & Caroline, Charlie, Jeremy & Alex, Alex B, Bec, Nat & Damon, Amanda and all the team at Beyond, Nicole & Michael and the team at LifeStyle Channel, Mary & Steve, Jen & Jeff, Sue & Fred, Wendy & Les, Helen & Vloster, Lyn & John, Nadine, Rachael, Chris and Alicia and everyone at Channel 9 and *The Block*.

Thank you to all my clients who have opened their doors, let me invade their lives and embraced change to allow them a home that they enjoy every day.

To the clients who allowed me to photograph their homes: Michelle & Steve, Liz & David, John & Alison, Sorelle & Brian, Mark & Elise, Angie & Michael, Linda, Andy & Michael.

To the team at Penguin – publisher Andrea McNamara, editor Daniel Hudspith and designer Laura Thomas – for being a dream to work with and being so patient and calm when my schedule was fast-tracking us to a derailing at deadline time.

My biggest thanks go to the most important people in my life. To my incredible husband, Steve, who supports and loves me in everything I do, and makes me smile everyday. To my biggest joys, Carly & Jess, thank you for choosing me to be your Mum and making me the proudest parent alive.

P.S. Thank you to Vanessa for your gorgeous photographs, Fo for waving your magic wand and Virginia for the beautiful flowers at all the shoots.

VIKING

Published by the Penguin Group
Penguin Group (Australia)
707 Collins Street, Melbourne, Victoria 3008, Australia
(a division of Pearson Australia Group Pty Ltd)
Penguin Group (USA) Inc.
375 Hudson Street, New York, New York 10014, USA
Penguin Group (Canada)
90 Eglinton Avenue East, Suite 700, Toronto, Canada ON M4P 2Y3
(a division of Pearson Penguin Canada Inc.)
Penguin Books Ltd
80 Strand, London WC2R 0RL England
Penguin Ireland
25 St Stephen's Green, Dublin 2, Ireland
(a division of Penguin Books Ltd)
Penguin Books India Pvt Ltd
11 Community Centre, Panchsheel Park, New Delhi – 110 017, India
Penguin Group (NZ)
67 Apollo Drive, Rosedale, North Shore 0632, New Zealand
(a division of Pearson New Zealand Ltd)
Penguin Books (South Africa) (Pty) Ltd
Rosebank Office Park, Block D, 181 Jan Smuts Avenue, Parktown North,
Johannesburg, 2196, South Africa
Penguin (Beijing) Ltd
7F, Tower B, Jiaming Center, 27 East Third Ring Road North, Chaoyang District,
Beijing 100020, China

Penguin Books Ltd, Registered Offices: 80 Strand, London, WC2R 0RL, England

First published by Penguin Group (Australia), 2013

10 9 8 7 6 5 4 3 2 1

Text and illustration copyright © Shaynna Blaze 2013
Cover and author photographs copyright © Greg Elms 2013
Photographs copyright © Vanessa Hall 2013,
except where otherwise acknowledged

The moral right of the author has been asserted

Cover and text design by Laura Thomas © Penguin Group (Australia)
Cover and author photographs by Greg Elms
Photographs by Vanessa Hall, except where otherwise acknowledged
Typeset in Garamond by Laura Thomas, Penguin Group (Australia)
Colour reproduction by Splitting Image, Clayton, Victoria
Printed and bound in China by Imago

National Library of Australia
Cataloguing-in-Publication data:

Blaze, Shaynna.
Design your home / Shaynna Blaze.
ISBN: 9780670076789 (pbk.)
Interior decoration

747

penguin.com.au

Picture Credits

Cover and author photographs by **Greg Elms**

All other photography by **Vanessa Hall** except:

Sampford IXL: pages 31 (right), 181 (top left)

Home Appliances (Elicia Collection): page 31 (left)

Albert Comper: pages 153 (top), 200, 201 (top right),
206 (centre), 209, 210 (bottom), 214 (bottom left), 215,
217 (bottom), 222 (top right)

Damon Wilder: pages 153 (bottom), 154 (bottom left)

Simon Wood Photography: 154 (bottom right), 156, 171
(bottom right), 172 (top), 174, 176 (top), 177, 181 (bottom
right), 186 (bottom right), 194, 195 (right), 196 (top), 212,
213 (top), 214 (bottom right)

Andy Jones: pages 220, 221

Patterns supplied by **Shutterstock**

The painting on pages xii and 11 is by David Bromley
(www.davidbromley.com)

The painting on pages 5 and 92 (bottom) is by Michael Johnson.